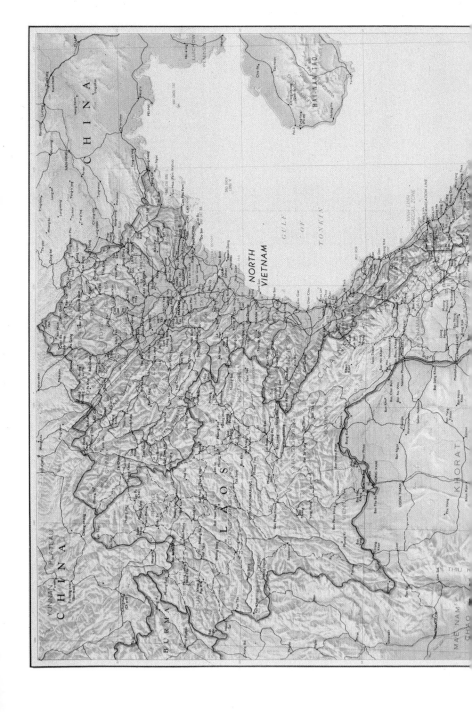

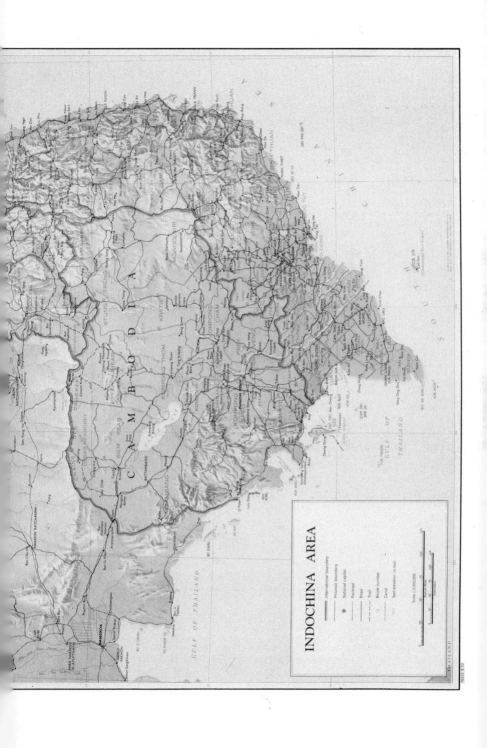

INDOCHINA AREA

International boundary
Province boundary
National capital
Railroad
Road
Trail
Route number
Canal
Spot elevation in feet

Scale 1:3,000,000

The Fall of South Vietnam

The Fall of South Vietnam

Statements *by* Vietnamese Military *and* Civilian Leaders

Stephen T. Hosmer
Konrad Kellen
Brian M. Jenkins

Crane, Russak & Company, Inc.

NEW YORK

BIBLIOGRAPHICAL NOTE

In view of the fact that the text of this book, with two minor exceptions, is based entirely on materials developed in personal contacts with the Vietnamese respondents who participated in this study, no books or other secondary sources on Vietnam were used. For this reason, this volume contains no bibliography.

The Fall of South Vietnam:
Statements by Vietnamese Military and Civilian Leaders

Published in the United States by
Crane, Russak & Company, Inc.
3 East 44th Street
New York, NY 10017

ISBN 0-8448-1345-1
Copyright © 1980 The Rand Corporation
Library of Congress Cataloging in Publication Data

Hosmer, Stephen T.
The Fall of South Vietnam.

"A Rand Corporation Research Study."
1. Vietnamese Conflict, 1961-1975.   I. Kellen, Konrad, joint author.
II. Jenkins, Brian Michael, joint author.   III. Title.
DS557.7.H68   1980   959.704'3   79-22805
ISBN 0-8448-1345-1

Printed in the United States of America

Contents

Chronology of
the Final Collapse

January 6	Capital of Phuoc Long province overrun by Communist forces.
March 4-7	Communist units cut major road networks in II Corps' highlands.
March 8-10	Communists initiate attacks on GVN positions in Quang Tri, Thua Thien, and Quang Tin provinces in I Corps.
March 10	I Corps ordered to begin redeployment of Airborne Division back to Saigon, which forces a compensating redeployment of Marine units from Quang Tri to the Danang area and triggers a mass exodus of refugees from Quang Tri and Hue.
	Communist armored and infantry units attack and occupy Ban Me Thuot. In following days, II Corps vainly attempts to mount a counterattack with 23d Division troops airlifted into Phuoc An.
March 11	President Thieu decides that a redeployment of forces is necessary to defend the most important areas of I and II Corps.
March 13	Thieu orders I Corps commander to develop plans for the redeployment of his forces to defend only the Danang area.
March 14	At a meeting at Cam Ranh Bay, Thieu orders the II Corps commander to rapidly "redeploy" forces from Pleiku and Kontum to the coast with the aim of eventually retaking Ban Me Thuot. Route 7B, a long-abandoned road, is selected as the withdrawal route.
March 16	Withdrawal of ARVN units from Pleiku and Kontum on Route 7B begins, but is soon stalled by need to repair bridges, enemy attacks, and the mass of civilian refugees clogging the road.

3

March 17	An airborne brigade withdrawn from I Corps is inserted near Khanh Duong in an attempt to stem Communist forces advancing from Ban Me Thuot toward the coast.
March 19	Thieu agrees to I Corps commander's alternative plan to regroup his forces into three enclaves at Hue, Danang, and Chu Lai.
March 20	I Corps commander receives instructions from JGS which he interprets as new orders to abandon Hue. Communists launch attacks south of Hue which threaten to cut route to Danang.
March 24	Communist armored column captures Tam Ky sealing off southern I Corps.
March 25	I Corps orders the evacuation of 1st Division and Marines from Hue to Danang and the 2d Division from Chu Lai to the offshore island of Cu Lao Re. Both operations largely fail.
March 29	Danang evacuated and I Corps falls.
April 1	Remnants of 22d Division evacuated from Qui Nhon, and II Corps staff flees Nha Trang. With exception of two most southeastern provinces, Communists control all of II Corps.
April 4	Prime Minister Khiem resigns.
April 7	Battle for Xuan Loc begins northeast of Saigon.
April 14	New government formed in Saigon. Can becomes Prime Minister.
April 16	Communist forces overrun reinforced ARVN units at Phan Rang airfield, capturing the last major GVN stronghold in II Corps.
April 21	Battle of Xuan Loc ends with withdrawal of 18th Division and other remaining defensive units. Saigon now ringed by 13 Communist divisions.
	President Thieu resigns in favor of Vice President Huong.
April 28	General ("Big") Minh becomes President.
April 30	President Minh surrenders unconditionally.

Vietnamese Personalities Mentioned in the Text

Ba, Ly Tong	Brigadier General, Commander of the 25th Infantry Division
Bao Dai	Last Emperor of Vietnam
Cam, Tran Van	Brigadier General, Assistant for Operations, II Corps
Can, Nguyen Ba	Speaker of the House and briefly Prime Minister in April 1975
Dang, Hoang Manh	Colonel, Chief of Staff, I Corps
Diem, Bui	Former Ambassador to the United States, and Adviser to President Thieu
Diem, Ngo Dinh	Former President of South Vietnam, 1955–1963
Don, Tran Van	Lieutenant General, former Chairman of Senate and House Defense Committees and briefly Minister of Defense in April 1975
Dung, Van Tien	North Vietnamese General, Member of the Politburo and Commander of North Vietnam's final offensive
Dzu, Ngo	Lieutenant General, former Commander of II Corps
Giap, Vo Nguyen	North Vietnamese General, Member of the Politburo and Minister of Defense
Hieu, Minh Van	Major General, former Commander of the 5th Infantry Division
Hinh, Nguyen Duy	Major General, Commander of the 3rd Infantry Division
Hung, Nguyen Tien	Minister of Planning
Huong, Tran Van	Vice President and successor to President Thieu in April 1975
Khanh, Nguyen	General, former Prime Minister and briefly President of South Vietnam in 1964
Khiem, Tran Thien	General, Prime Minister and Minister of Defense under President Thieu, 1970–1975
Khuyen, Dong Van	Lieutenant General, Chief of Staff, Joint General Staff, and Commander Central Logistics Command
Ky, Nguyen Cao	Air Vice Marshal, former Commander of the Air Force, Premier, and Vice President; without official command in 1975.
Lam, Hoang Xuan	Lieutenant General, former Commander of I Corps

Lan, Bui The	Major General, Commander of the Marine Division
Loan, Pham Ky	Colonel, Deputy Commander of the Central Logistics Command
Loc, Vinh	Lieutenant General, briefly assumed duties of Chairman of the Joint General Staff, April 1975
Loi, Nguyen Huy	Colonel, former Adviser to the South Vietnamese Delegation to the Paris Talks and Special Assistant to the Inspector General, Joint General Staff, and to the Capital Military District Commander
Ly, Le Khac	Colonel, Chief of Staff, II Corps
Minh, Duong Van	General, last President of South Vietnam, April 1975
Minh, Tran Van	Lieutenant General, Commander of the Air Force
Nam, Nguyen Khoa	Major General, Commander of IV Corps
Nha, Hoang Duc	Former Minister of Information, cousin and close personal adviser to President Thieu
Nhan, Do Ngoc	Colonel, Joint General Staff officer
Niem, Phan Diem	Major General, Commander of the 22d Infantry Division
Phu, Pham Van	Major General, Commander of II Corps
Phuong, Tran Kim	Ambassador to the United States
Quang, Dang Van	Lieutenant General, Special Assistant for Military and Security Affairs to President Thieu
Quang, Vu The	Colonel, Deputy Commander of the 23d Infantry Division
Sang, Pham Ngoc	Brigadier General, Commander of the 6th Air Division
Tat, Pham Duy	Brigadier General, Commander of the Rangers in II Corps
Thanh, Father Tran Huu	Leader of the "Anti-Corruption" Movement
Thieu, Nguyen Van	President of South Vietnam, 1967–1975
Thinh, Nguyen Xuan	Lieutenant General, Commander of the Artillery Command
Thuc, Truong Tan	Colonel, Deputy Commander of 1st Infantry Division
Touneh, Hantho	Secretary General, Ministry for the Development of Ethnic Minorities, Montagnard Leader
Tra, Tran Van	North Vietnamese General, Head of the Viet Cong Delegation in the Joint Military Commission in Saigon
Truong, Ngo Quang	Lieutenant General, Commander of I Corps
Tuong, Le Trung	Brigadier General, Commander of the 23d Infantry Division
Uoc, .Vu Van	Colonel, Commander, Air Operations Command, VNAF
Vien, Buu	Assistant Minister of Defense, Secretary of State to the Prime Minister's Office, and briefly Minister of Interior
Vien, Cao Van	General, Chairman of the Joint General Staff

6

Preface

This report is a summary of extensive oral and written statements by twenty-seven former high-ranking South Vietnamese military officers and civilians on their perceptions of the causes of the collapse of South Vietnam in the spring of 1975. These statements were obtained by the authors of this report, for the most part in 1976. The study was done for the Historian, Office of the Secretary of Defense.

We have tried to summarize what the respondents said, without evaluating their statements. The reader in turn is urged to keep in mind that the views summarized and the recollections given are those of the South Vietnamese respondents. When presenting a summary such as this in narrative form, it is difficult to avoid creating the impression from time to time that the views expressed are those of the authors, if only because a view found worth quoting is often a view shared. But that is not the case here, whether or not the authors might happen to agree with some of the points expressed. In short, should the reader find himself at any point agreeing or disagreeing with what is stated in these pages, he is reminded that he is agreeing or disagreeing with former South Vietnamese officials, not with the authors.

However one might judge the validity of the views of the respondents, they do point up the many obstacles in the way of effective communication between allies of vastly different cultures and strengths. Thus, studies of this kind can have more than mere historical interest.

Summary

In the view of twenty-seven former high-ranking South Vietnamese officers and civilians who were asked by the authors about their perceptions of the reasons for the sudden collapse of South Vietnam in 1975, there were about a half-dozen principal causes. A number of these root causes were traced to grievous shortcomings in South Vietnam's politico-military leadership, planning, and organization; the respondents found much to criticize in their own institutions and behavior both during the period leading up to and throughout the course of the collapse itself. However, in one way or another, they also perceived these causes to be all interrelated and in turn all tied to what the South Vietnamese officials regarded as the overarching cause for the debacle: the American role in the drama.

This role had two distinct aspects or phases, in their minds. Before the Paris Agreements, the American role was seen as that of a gigantic but somewhat blind and often oppressive "super-ally" who did not clearly understand the nature of the war, the nature of the South Vietnamese society, the nature of the enemy, or the needs of South Vietnam if it was ever to become socially viable and militarily able to face the enemy at the same time. Then, after the Paris Agreements, the American role, in their estimation, took the form of a rather callous and incomprehensible "abandonment" of South Vietnam; in fact, to all of them, the signing of the Paris Agreements themselves signified and symbolized that very "abandonment" which they felt was primarily responsible for the defeat of 1975.

With regard to that perceived abandonment, the persons interviewed stressed that the physical side of it—the withdrawal of troops, the loss of U.S. airpower, declining aid—was no more disastrous than the concomitant psychological effects of no longer being regarded by the United States as worth saving. They regarded the decline in aid, particularly in the face of the ever-growing might of their enemy and the support that the enemy received from *his* allies, as irrefutable proof.

At the same time—and this is not as paradoxical as it might appear—their confidence in the United States was such that, according to them, it too actually contributed to the sudden collapse, having led them to conduct their military and civilian affairs with considerable complacency. The pillar under this unquestioning faith in U.S. help in an emergency was their conviction that the United States could and would "do something" if the enemy were to undertake cease-fire violations of such magnitude as to upset the balance and seriously endanger their national existence. They had, or said they had, the solemn assurances of five American presidents that they would receive such aid in an emergency; these assurances included that of President Ford who, two days after ascending to the presidency, had written a letter to Thieu reaffirming the policy of all his predecessors. Most of all, the South Vietnamese had had their belief that the United States would not permit their conquest confirmed by what President Nixon had told them at San Clemente in 1973 and communicated to them later.

They believed implicitly in these assurances, they said, not just because the assurances had been made orally and in writing by five U.S. presidents, but also because they were convinced that U.S. self-interest would never allow the absorption of South Vietnam into the Communist world. The very fact that the United States had entered the war on such a scale and had borne such heavy sacrifices was regarded as proof positive that the United States considered the independence of South Vietnam vital to its own security interest and would enter the war directly, at least with strong contingents of B-52s and other airpower, if that should be needed. The respondents relied all the more on the United States, despite their feelings of being abandoned, as their own strategic options did not permit successful termination of the war even theoretically and under the best of circumstances. The enemy, they always felt, "would never give up"—which is in considerable contrast with some long-held U.S. perceptions that if the war were made too expensive for the enemy, in casualties, for example, he would eventually desist. The mere fact that, for so many reasons, the South Vietnamese could not go North, whereas the enemy could go South, was symbolic, in their view, of the strategic box in which they found themselves; the withdrawal of American air-power permitted the enemy to prepare for a knock-out blow (through a buildup of lines of communication and force concentrations) which they could never hope to either spoil while it was in the making or meet when it fell, without direct U.S. military intervention in Vietnam and/or U.S. diplomatic intervention in Moscow and Peking.

It was also the American role, in the view of the respondents, that dissuaded them from cleaning their own house or at least effectively trying to do so while there still seemed to be time. The Americans, they said, misreading the war and the enemy, had saddled them with a military organization ill-suited to meet the enemy after the Paris Agreements and impossible to maintain with declining aid. The South Vietnamese soldier had been "conditioned" by the U.S. presence to rely on vast air and artillery support in combat and had "forgotten how to walk," being used to motorized and air transportation—military resources that became increasingly scarce after 1972. Furthermore, many respondents felt that ARVN (the Army of the Republic of Vietnam) had been organized along the wrong pattern: It had far too big a "tail," and it lacked the mobile reserve divisions essential to counter a conventional North Vietnamese assault. Compounding these problems was the absence of a viable command and planning structure within the South Vietnamese armed forces (the Americans had all too willingly dominated these functions during their presence) and the lack of effective military leadership at the top, many senior officers having received their appointments for reasons of political loyalty or through linkages of corruption rather than military competence. On the civilian side, corruption and inflation had taken their toll in national will and military morale. Because of accumulated grievances, the political base of the Thieu regime had

11

eroded to the point where the country was on the brink of political chaos. True, this had to a large extent been the result of bad national leadership before and after Paris; but that bad leadership, in their estimation, had been at least in part the result of American influence and pressure, particularly what seemed to them the unconditional U.S. support for Thieu.

The *suddenness* of the actual collapse under the enemy offensive of 1975 was attributed by the respondents to several factors. One was the adverse balance of forces that existed by 1975. Since the signing of the Paris Agreements, North Vietnam had greatly strengthened the quantity and quality of its offensive capabilities in the South, and because of its improved logistics networks was able to rapidly concentrate forces (including armor and artillery) and attack South Vietnamese points of weakness almost at will. The ARVN, on the other hand, had been weakened by continued casualties and desertions and by the reduction of supplies resulting from the decline in American aid and was spread extremely thin throughout the country in an effort to protect widespread territories. Another factor in the collapse was the element of surprise: Even the most pessimistic among the South Vietnamese had not expected a full-scale, general offensive because they thought—and thought the enemy thought—that the United States would actively intervene in such a case, and that this would prevent the North Vietnamese from undertaking it. Once the offensive got under way and—to the surprise of the enemy—proceeded with so little opposition from South Vietnam's armed forces, the principal weaknesses of the South Vietnamese structure became apparent; the absence of defense plans, especially plans for strategic retreats, led to catastrophic losses in military assets and morale immediately after the fall of Ban Me Thuot, the target of the offensive's first major (and successful) attack.

Next among the fatal weaknesses as perceived by the respondents and brought to light by the events of 1975 was the lack of a mobile reserve (that had long been an item of dispute and anxiety but not of action in Saigon), and the lack of strategic mobility in general, due to shortages of fuel, transport, and spares. Then there was the weakness, if not virtual absence, of a functioning general staff; inadequate leadership and insufficient technical training on the part of local commanders; ubiquitous ammunition shortages; and poor intelligence. There was a breakdown in military and political leadership, attributed by the respondents primarily to Thieu. Also seen as important was the fact that the fighting in I and II Corps took place in areas inhabited by the dependents of soldiers who deserted en masse to save their families or at least be with them. This led to a total breakdown of discipline, morale, and resistance, as in Danang, where some crack troops not only failed to defend but actually mutinied.

Another disastrous factor appears to have been irresolution and violent reversal of strategy at the top. Until the big onslaught from the North, Thieu's strategy had been to hold on to every outpost, even though this had dispersed and chewed up his forces; he now reversed himself in a series of sudden strategic redeployments that virtually precluded an organized defense. He sacrificed too much too fast, handing the enemy the entire northern part of South Vietnam and thereby making their victory inevitable, according to the sources. The quick retreats from the northern territories, aside from being strategically disastrous, had also led to widespread rumors among the people that a "deal" had been made between North and South (and perhaps between Washington and Moscow) whereby a new partitioning of Vietnam further south was to occur. This rumor—possibly started but at least fanned by the enemy— triggered a massive flight of civilian refugees that disrupted military movements and further induced the soldiers not to fight, for why fight if a "deal" had been made?

Finally, commanders were reported not to have stuck with their troops but to have abandoned them in critical situations, thereby deepening the disorganization and panic. During the final weeks, most of the senior South Vietnamese military and civilian leadership at both the Corps and national level suffered from a paralysis of inactivity, a condition characterized by the respondents as one where "no one was in charge of anything . . . no one did anything." All these factors together led to "a rout unprecedented in the annals of military history," as one South Vietnamese general put it, despite sporadic heroic resistance of some ARVN units. The

South Vietnamese leaders, apparently including Thieu himself, then kept hoping for the United States to come to their rescue until the very end. Last but not least, they regarded it as axiomatic that nothing of basic importance in their country or even in the world could happen without U.S. volition or sanction.

From a different angle, however, quite a few respondents regarded the events in South Vietnam as inexorable, more so perhaps than did Western observers, who often attributed the fall of that country to one or two relatively simple and theoretically remediable reasons. The sources sometimes said, on the one hand, when dwelling on the corruption, lethargy, and gross mismanagement of human, economic, and military resources, "We defeated ourselves." Yet, at the same time, when asked whether under different conditions or with different actions the outcome might have been different, most of them replied, "Only if the U.S. had not abandoned us." Thus, they said that if they had not suffered from grievous errors on the battlefield, or lack of ordnance and transport, or whatever, "they would have gained some time." But when asked how much time that would have been and how this would have affected things, all but one or two respondents said that it would at best have gained them a few months, after which all would have depended on direct American intervention, most notably with B-52s. Such American intervention, in the view of a considerable portion of the respondents, would have been more likely to be forthcoming after a few more months of resistance, which would have given the South Vietnamese a chance to "prove themselves" and thereby more or less force the Americans to come to the rescue of their ally.

Some of the respondents attributed the defeat of South Vietnam to fundamental aspects in the struggle between East and West. They felt that in this fight, Communism had the edge, partly because the democratic side—their side—was in a dilemma: If it granted democratic freedoms in times of deadly war, it had to lose for lack of discipline; and if it was a dictatorship, well, then the people perhaps did not consider it worth fighting for.

As for Vietnamization, the respondents had mainly negative comments. It had come too late and too abruptly; it had been superimposed on a South Vietnamese military and civilian structure that was ill-equipped to absorb it; and it was frankly regarded by some as a mere fig leaf over the "abandonment" which the respondents regarded as central to the defeat. Those respondents who believed that alternate military strategies or organization could have made a significant difference thought that Vietnamization would have had to be much more far-reaching and much more vigorous and would have had to occur years earlier to allow an effective transfer of the burden; in their view, the Americans, while they were in Vietnam, had exerted much too much influence over the South Vietnamese to allow political institutions and military leadership to come into their own, then or later.

Regardless of what the respondents saw as the causes of the collapse, they tended to stress that unsuccessful U.S.-South Vietnamese interaction had been largely responsible for it. They stated that misunderstandings, misperceptions, and the tendency to engage in counterproductive practices had been entirely mutual. They pointed to the curious paradox that whereas the American presence had been regarded by them as oppressive and stultifying in some respects, the American departure after 1972 had left a crippling vacuum in the command structure and had an adverse psychological effect as well. Some said that to the extent that it succeeded at all, U.S.-South Vietnamese interaction had been more effective on the lower than on the higher military levels. Others said that they did not envy the American leaders who had to deal with the kind of Vietnamese people in power in Saigon and in the Joint General Staff (JGS), but they believed that the low caliber of South Vietnamese leadership was to some extent the result of American influence. None left any doubt that in their view the alliance between the biggest and most powerful nation of the West and the small, technologically undeveloped Asian nation had been a failure.

Acknowledgments

The authors wish to express their indebtedness to Bui Diem, former Republic of Vietnam Ambassador to Washington, and Buu Vien, former Assistant Minister of Defense in the South Vietnamese Government and (briefly) Minister of the Interior. Both of these men, by providing much factual information and analytical thought, contributed substantially in long discussions with the authors.

Appreciation is hereby expressed to Paul F. Langer and George K. Tanham of Rand, who made a number of very helpful suggestions for improving this report. The reading of an early draft by Bernard Brodie, Arnold Horelick, Nathan Leites, and Guy J. Pauker also yielded useful advice. Appreciation is also expressed to Janet DeLand for her fine editorial assistance.

The authors also wish to acknowledge the help they received at the outset of the project from Brigadier General James L. Collins, Jr., Chief of Military History, United States Army, and Lieutenant General William D. Potts (Ret.), of the General Research Corporation, in the form of invaluable information on where and how to find the most promising respondents.

Throughout the effort, the support of (then) Deputy Assistant Secretary of Defense Morton I. Abramowitz, and the Historian, Office of the Secretary of Defense, Dr. Alfred Goldberg, has been of great help to the authors.

Finally, the authors acknowledge their debt to Lilita Dzirkals, also of Rand, for furnishing historical information which facilitated the interviewing. Mary L. Sauters, Susanne Farmer, and Carolyn P. Dooley labored patiently and well on the typing of the voluminous manuscript. Susanne and Mary also provided invaluable help throughout the course of the project.

Introduction

When the Republic of South Vietnam collapsed in April 1975 under the massive enemy offensive launched in the course of that year, most, if not all, observers of the events were surprised by the swiftness and completeness of South Vietnam's disintegration. As we now know from enemy sources, even Hanoi's leaders were surprised. According to their own statements, they had been prepared and expecting to fight well into 1976, the year of the presidential election in the United States.

Actually, the collapse took even less time than the period that passed between the launching of the last offensive in early March and the unconditional surrender of Saigon on April 30. The military fate of South Vietnam really was sealed in about 20 days: from the attack on Ban Me Thuot on March 10 until the fall of Danang on March 29. Everything else was just prelude and final denouement. Significantly enough, even those 20 days saw no single decisive battle. No Dien Bien Phu. There were only some fierce, isolated engagements, some other contacts with the enemy here and there, and, on the whole, unsuccessful attempts at redeploying forces. There was panic, disorder, tragic numbers of military and civilian casualties by unopposed enemy fire and even by friendly air power; and there were mass desertions, mutiny, and flight—in brief, a rout "unique in the annals of military history," as one South Vietnamese general put it. "As a matter of fact," added this general, "everything was unique in the closing days of the Vietnam war: There were three presidents in one week, a one-million-man army was annihilated in two months, five billion dollars worth of equipment was lost, a country with nineteen million people collapsed and joined the ranks of the Communist countries, and the Bamboo Curtain fell on this once rich and beautiful land.''

As soon as the sudden and complete collapse had become history, views and theories as to its causes sprang up everywhere. In late 1975, the Office of the Secretary of Defense asked The Rand Corporation to conduct interviews with a number of leading Vietnamese military men (and some civilian leaders, as well) who had taken refuge in the United States. The mission was to elicit from these men their personal recollections of what they had seen and done during the critical period and what they perceived as the principal causes of the suddenness of the collapse—and to do this before memories dimmed and mythology set in. Rand researchers thereupon contacted some of these former leaders and found most of them ready, indeed eager, to dwell at great length on the events as they saw them.

In the course of the effort, twenty-seven former Vietnamese leaders were interviewed, and eleven were asked to write essays as well. This report summarizes and quotes from these interviews and essays. Of the twenty-seven respondents who participated in this effort, twenty-three were high-ranking officers and four were civilians. The military group consisted of South Vietnam's former Premier, Air Marshal Nguyen Cao Ky; thirteen general officers (including eight lieutenant generals); and nine colonels. About half of these officers held key combat commands; the other half held senior staff positions. All had participated in the war for many years, and most had served in a variety of important positions during the course of their careers. Among them were men such as the Minister of Defense during Saigon's final days, the commanders of I Corps and the Capital Military District, the Chief of Staff of II Corps, and the Commanding General, Artillery Command.

The military officials were selected mainly on the basis of (1) their presence in critical areas of interest, such as I Corps and II Corps and the region around Saigon; (2) their experience in such areas as air, artillery, training, and operations, and the Joint General Staff (JGS); and (3) their accessibility. The civilian officials were selected on the basis of their knowledge of South Vietnamese government operations. No officer from III or IV

Corps, the Airborne Division, or the Navy was included, because of time and resource constraints and lack of availability. All respondents were interviewed during the twelve-month period from February 1976 to January 1977.

The civilian officials who participated in this study were Bui Diem, former Republic of Vietnam Ambassador to Washington and adviser to President Nguyen Van Thieu; Buu Vien, formerly Assistant Minister of Defense and (briefly) Minister of the Interior and a close adviser to Prime Minister Tran Thien Khiem; Nguyen Ba Can, Speaker of the House from 1971 and Prime Minister in the month of April 1975; and Hantho Touneh, a Montagnard official in the Ministry for the Development of Ethnic Minorities.

Unfortunately, we were unable to obtain President Nguyen Van Thieu's views, as he declined to talk with us directly or through others.

It should be emphasized that the military and civilian officials who cooperated in this study constitute only a limited portion of South Vietnam's command structure. Are the respondents selected by the authors, then, representative of that structure? By the end of the war, South Vietnam had an estimated 350 high-ranking officers (full colonel to four-star general), approximately 100 of whom held key commands or key staff positions. About 70 of these are reported to have reached the United States. Of these, 23 were interviewed in the course of this effort. As already pointed out, the interviewees were selected on the basis of having witnessed and participated in the most important actions, i.e., those in I and II Corps, or of having had a full overview, as members of the JGS or other important commands. Many of the key participants remained in Vietnam or were unavailable for interview. How their perceptions might have differed from those quoted here is unknown. However, although these men could undoubtedly add many important details of their perceptions of the fundamental causes of the collapse, there is no reason to assume that they would say anything that would significantly alter the picture.

The interviews were conducted in English, as most of the interviewees were proficient in the language. Translators had to be used in only three instances. The setting was relatively informal: Almost half of the respondents were interviewed at their homes, and the remainder at Rand or at other offices.

The interviewers did not use a set questionnaire. As guidance for their interviews they relied primarily on the following objectives: to learn from each respondent his personal part in the final stages of the war, as well as his thoughts and observations; to have him express what, in his view, were the primary causes of the debacle; and to have him speak frankly on U.S.-Vietnamese relations. An attempt was made to probe important issues in considerable detail, and many of the interviews required a full day to complete.

The reader may ask whether the authors have selected quotations from the sources in a reasonably representative manner, given the fact that most of the quotes, whether they deal with U.S.-Vietnamese cooperation, military aid, leadership, or strategy, are on the negative side. It is reasonable to ask, Did the respondents not have anything positive to report? Or, if they did, did the authors deliberately neglect to quote such positive statements? In a word, is this a balanced account? And if not, why not? The answer is that the basic question addressed to the sources was, *Why was the collapse so sudden and so complete?* Inevitably, this established a context for the responses in which the perceived causes of the collapse, i.e., negative features, had to predominate.

How were the quotes actually selected from the basic materials? During the interviews, the respondents were asked questions about their perceptions regarding some of the major events that are common knowledge, such as the fall of Danang and the rout of the retreating forces in II Corps; and each interviewee was asked to report on what he had observed, done, and thought about in his particular post. In similar fashion, the writers of the report focused on topics as they emerged from the materials and *then selected those comments which seemed most illustrative of the factors stressed by the respondents.* Where there were deviating opinions on major issues, such opinions were included.

Despite the apparent candor with which the interviewees responded, they did not, presumably, respond without *bias*. On the whole, this bias—as would be expected—runs in the direction of exonerating themselves and placing the blame primarily on what they regarded as poor leadership on the part of others, particularly at the top in Saigon, and on the United States for failing to support South Vietnam more extensively after the Paris Agreements or to come directly to its aid in 1975. All of the respondents also severely criticized the Paris Agreements themselves. Whether or not such "frankness" with the investigators can be regarded as evidence that the respondents were candid is not certain. But in general the respondent who is critical is more likely to be candid.

Some of the broader statements by the respondents, for example, their views on leadership, are not simple facts that can be checked; other statements, such as those concerning alleged shortages or certain U.S. actions, are subject to verification. But the authors have *not* examined the content of such statements by comparing them to U.S. sources, because the purpose of this study was to obtain the views of the Vietnamese and try to learn what *they* thought.

In the text, some of the quotations have been attributed to respondents by name and others have not. Those not identified were taken from statements that the respondents did not wish to have attributed to them or from statements by respondents who did not wish to be identified at all.

This report is unique in that it presents the views of the South Vietnamese military and, to a much lesser extent, civilian leadership on the collapse of South Vietnam. Of course, the study of the events is by no means complete. For example, interviews with lower-ranking South Vietnamese soldiers would provide comments from a different perspective. Or the province chiefs and district commanders who dealt with the civilian population might offer still another set of views. Last but not least, interviews with key American officials might challenge some of the statements quoted in this report.

One thing most of the respondents agreed on: No single calamitous event or mistake can be held responsible for the collapse of South Vietnam. And none of them stated that the enemy's military power was so overwhelming that all resistance was futile, even though many came close to that by saying that resistance without active help from the United States was futile against an offensive of such proportions as the enemy mounted in 1975. Yet some of the respondents stated, at the same time, that they "defeated themselves," although they attributed a considerable share of the responsibility to the United States, for a wide variety of reasons.

Regardless of where the South Vietnamese officials saw the causes, in most of their accounts the general situation in South Vietnam before the collapse was described as so precarious that the configuration of military and political factors before the collapse must be regarded as an integral part of the events. According to the respondents, the patient did not die of the blows he was dealt so much as of his anterior vulnerability to those blows. As one senior diplomat put it:

> Although the collapse of April 1975 could not be considered in absolute terms as an inevitable consequence of these mistakes, the situation in South Vietnam at the beginning of 1975 was such that a simple error could turn a dangerous situation into an irretrievable one, and that was exactly what happened.

In their accounts, the respondents often went back in time, at least to the conclusion of the Paris Agreements of January 1973.

The first part of this report, then, is devoted to the situation up to the beginning of the 1975 offensive. The second part deals with the course of the collapse.

The causes of the collapse, as the sources saw them, are so many and so inextricably interwoven that it is difficult to present them in linear fashion. Therefore, the subdivision of Part I into its seven chapters is at times quite arbitrary. As most things mentioned by the respondents are causally connected with almost everything else, what we have put into one chapter could often just as well have appeared in the next.

PART I
The Setting Before
The 1975
Enemy Offensive

Chapter 1

The Paris Agreements and the Decline of U.S. Support

The Paris Agreements and the Decline of U.S. Support

All of the respondents began their explanations of the course and causes of the sudden collapse of South Vietnam by going back in time to the situation that prevailed in South Vietnam prior to the final big enemy offensive in 1975. And most of them sooner or later talked about the Paris Agreements of 1973, which they regarded as one of the turning points in the war—a turning point for the worse.

The Paris Agreements

Bui Diem, Saigon's Ambassador to Washington from 1967 to 1972, reported:

> I still remember the words of President Thieu when I saw him a few weeks before the signing of the Paris Agreements and received his instructions for one of my frequent trips to the U.S. as his special emissary to watch over the peace negotiations: "Go to Washington and Paris and try and do your best. To raise again at this hour the problem of the North Vietnamese troops on our territory is perhaps too late, but as long as we still have a chance to improve the Agreements we have to try. If we cannot now obtain the basic requirements for our survival, things will be very difficult for us in the long run. And the withdrawal of the North Vietnamese troops is one of the basic requirements."

29

According to his testimony, Bui Diem then did try his best but was not successful. Particularly distressing, according to him, was a series of responses from President Nixon. Diem reported:

> The final decision by Saigon to sign the Agreements came after a rather painful exchange of messages between Presidents Nixon and Thieu—almost every day during the week prior to signing—with some of the messages from President Nixon couched in the toughest language that diplomatic practice has ever seen: "I am firmly convinced that the alternative to signing the present agreement is a total cut-off of funds to assist your country" . . . "If you refuse to join us, the responsibility for the consequences rests on the government of South Vietnam" . . . "If you cannot give me a positive answer by 1200 Washington time, January 21, 1973, I shall authorize Dr. Kissinger to initial the agreement even without the concurrence of your government."

Even more pernicious than the Agreements themselves, according to respondents, was the fact that violations of the Agreements were tolerated by the United States. One respondent stated pointedly, "The only provision of the Paris Agreements that was observed was the removal of foreign troops from Vietnam, namely American troops."

Others had similar comments. One general who held a leading position in I Corps stated:

> If the Paris Agreements were already bad and led to a situation where both sides fought each other viciously to control more land and more people, the ICCS [International Commission for Control and Supervision], which was set up to enforce the armistice, not only failed to do its job but was beset by the bickering among its members and—far worse—apparently served as a listening and spying post for its Communist members. In fact, every day one could see Hungarians and Poles go freely around, snapping pictures at airports, bridges, and military installations. They had direct radio communications with Hanoi . . . whenever the Poles and Hungarians withdrew from certain areas, it was expected that these places would soon be attacked.

What also allegedly distressed some South Vietnamese was the American attitude toward Communist members of the Commission:

> One story which made the cocktail circuit in Saigon had it that after VC General Tran Van Tra, head of the VC delegation who in 1968 had directed the Tet offensive in Saigon and became military governor of Saigon after the war, expressed his love of classical music, the Americans presented him the next day with a set of stereo with all paraphernalia of loudspeakers and assorted records of classical music.

That the Paris Agreements were continuously violated by the enemy did not come as a surprise to the South Vietnamese (who committed some violations of their own). However, in their estimation there was a disproportion in the significance of these violations, in that every violation of the Agreements by the enemy, beyond its immediate effect or purpose, represented a challenge to the United States and a test as to whether or how the United States would respond. And the fact that the United States did not respond to the violations apparently depressed and worried the South Vietnamese leaders more than the violations themselves. Lack of U.S. response was one of the reasons why the Vietnamese, as they put it, felt "abandoned" after the conclusion of the Agreements, a term that recurs frequently in their statements.

Many respondents regarded the Paris Agreements as the fundamental cause of the collapse. Among the major disadvantages that accrued to the Government of South Vietnam (GVN) from the Agreements, the following were cited: (1) the in-place cease-fire, which made its area of control vulnerable to Communist "land grab" tactics and made military difficulties for the GVN; (2) the fact that the Agreements left North Vietnamese troops in South Vietnamese territory; and (3) the political disadvantages, particularly the clause calling for the establishment of a Committee of Concord and National Reconciliation, which gave the Communists too much legitimacy.

The Enhance Operation and Aid in General

The Paris Agreements were associated in the minds of the South Vietnamese leaders with more than violations by the enemy and lack of U.S. response. Even though U.S. troop withdrawals had been almost completed when the Agreements were signed, they somehow ratified the departure of American arms. And even though the Agreements *per se* did not in practice seriously constrain U.S. aid, the decline of that aid in the years after the signing seems associated in the minds of Vietnamese leaders with the Agreements themselves, perhaps because aid in the form of the Enhance Operation was used, as some of the respondents stated, to induce them to sign.

When asked about the Enhance resupply efforts that preceded the signing of the Paris Agreements, a high-ranking officer responded that the equipment provided was not of much use and most of it stayed in storage. He said that the Enhance effort was a political ploy to establish a basis for a one-for-one replacement program later on and was also mounted as an inducement for the GVN to sign the Paris Agreements. Citing examples of dubious equipment, the officer mentioned the problems ARVN had with the C-130s they were given. He said that of the 32 aircraft they received, only about 8 to 12 could fly on any given day.

Another high-ranking officer, a general in the JGS, had an almost identical view of the Enhance Operation. While noting that some of this materiel had been used to activate some new units, it was his belief that the Enhance Operation was laid on to reassure President Thieu about continued U.S. support and to convince him to sign the Paris Agreements. He noted the fact that much of the equipment was secondhand (the F-5s which were provided by South Korea and Taiwan) and that South Vietnam later had to pay for this equipment out of its U.S. aid allotment.

But the Enhance Operation was only a part of the supply and aid situation in general. Summing up, the general said that "the lack of adequate military aid to South Vietnam following the Paris Agreements of 1973 was the second fundamental cause of the collapse" (the first being the Agreements themselves).

32

Commenting on the subject of supplies, former Ambassador Bui Diem stated:

The "tightening of the screw" period began right [after the Paris Agreements]. Persistent antiwar feelings [in the United States], illusions of peace generated by the peace agreement, [American] antipathy against the one-man regime in Saigon—all these factors resulted in the fact that the South Vietnamese received during the calendar year 1973 barely what they needed for their survival. And this was but the beginning of the trend, because the real difficulties came only in 1974 when an unfortunate confluence of reverses came along:

1. Of a requested $1.6 billion in military aid, the U.S. Congress appropriated only $700 million (in spite of the fact that an earlier bill had already authorized $1 billion).

2. An unexpected action by the DoD, charging off $300 million worth of equipment against FY 1975 (while normally it should have been charged against FY 1974), thus further reducing the volume of military aid to $400 million.

3. Economic aid being almost totally consumed by soaring costs of fuel and commodities in the world market.

4. An urgent request for additional aid which was ignored by a U.S. Congress too much absorbed by Watergate, and, most important of all,

5. The resignation of Mr. Nixon, who was considered rightly or wrongly as the solid supporter of Mr. Thieu and of the anti-Communist cause.

Concerning Enhance, Bui Diem had this to say:

This . . . costly equipment was considered at the time as a gesture from the U.S. Administration to induce the Thieu government to sign the Agreements. It had perhaps its political value—practically everything which could be construed as a form of guarantee from the U.S. not to abandon South Vietnam was welcomed by Mr. Thieu. But it was hastily and ill-conceived, and the whole program had little military value; in fact a lot of this equipment could not be effectively used by the South Vietnamese armed forces who later

33

complained that they needed men and money just for the maintenance of this unusable equipment.

And Bui Diem concluded his observations on diminishing aid:

These [problems], quite naturally, had immediate and dangerous effect on the situation in Vietnam: The already fragile economic and social stability of the country was seriously affected, signs of political instability began to appear and the South Vietnamese armed forces were forced to reduce their activities to a critical minimum, leaving the field free to their enemies. But topping it all, in a sort of cumulative effect, there was the psychological impact provoked by the succession of bad news which in turn created an atmosphere of uncertainty in Saigon during the final months of 1974 and caused the collapse of the morale of the whole South Vietnamese regime.

According to battlefield commanders, the effects of reduced aid were having a serious impact on their operations. One I Corps general stated:

It went without saying that the lack of supplies and adequate fire support resulted in a dramatic increase in the rate of casualties. Military hospitals were overcrowded . . . they were critically short in medicines, especially dextrose, antibiotics, and also plasma. . . . As a result the combat units saw their ranks rapidly depleted and were hard put to replace their losses. As a matter of fact, in 1975 no infantry battalion ever had more than 400 men . . . and a Ranger battalion no more than 300. The recruiting operations became more difficult, while the desertion rate increased. All of these, added to the increasing economic difficulties, were having a devastating effect on the morale of the army and the country as well, and were a major cause in their final collapse.

According to this general, Med-Evac operations were also affected:

In Saigon, the ambulance units were so short in gasoline that in order to evacuate the wounded, they had to tow four ambulances in a row with a 2½-ton truck . . . even worse, a wounded soldier sometimes had to wait for the company of two or three more of his comrades to be worth an evacuation by ambulance, and many unnecessarily died this way.

Long-time Speaker of the House and short-term Prime Minister (in 1975) Nguyen Ba Can had this to say on the subject of aid:

> The deep cause of the surrender must be attributed first to the Vietnamese defects, such as government inefficiency, the loss of the people's confidence, the declining morale of the armed forces, and secondly to the disastrous cutoff of vital military aid.

Actually, the decline in aid was regarded as possibly necessitating drastic strategy realignments. One staff officer, discussing the problems created by the cutbacks in U.S. military aid, said that he and other members of the JGS had speculated from time to time about the amount of South Vietnam's territory that could be defended with differing amounts of U.S. military aid. He said that they had run a rough mathematical exercise and concluded that with $1.5 billion in military aid they would be able to defend all four Corps areas, but with only $700 million they would be able to defend only III and IV Corps. He said the results of this exercise were discussed with Prime Minister Khiem, General Vien, Chairman of the JGS, General Khuyen, and even with President Thieu. However, even with the $1.5 billion, they said, it would have been very difficult to hold South Vietnam without U.S. air and naval support. As to the amount of stocks actually available in South Vietnam in the spring of 1975, the officer estimated that the munitions and other materials on hand would have allowed South Vietnam to continue its defense only until about May or June.

Vietnamization

If some leading personalities in South Vietnam did not feel good about U.S. aid in the days before the last enemy offensive, they did not feel good about Vietnamization either. General Tran Van Don, I Corps Commander in the 1960s, former Chairman of the Senate

35

and House Defense Committees, and, finally, Minister of Defense, had this to say:

> I was an opponent of Vietnamization . . . I will tell just one story. I visited [some units in the field] and tried to understand the program of Vietnamization of the war . . . it was in the headquarters of the 5th Division. I discussed the question with the commander of the division, General Minh Van Hieu, a most honest general, and capable, too. I was surprised by his answer; it opened my eyes. I asked him, "What do you think of Vietnamization?" He said to me, "It is impossible to be implemented." Why? He said, "The 5th Division covers an area where there were two other divisions, Americans, and now with the departure of the two American divisions I have only my division to cover the whole area. I have three regiments for this area and must use one regiment to replace one division. How can I face the enemy like this? I have become weaker." He looked very disappointed. I was surprised; he was a quiet man, a polite man, and he tried to do his best. But he said to me that this was impossible. "How can I cover a bigger area with less units?" So the Vietnamization of the war means that we are becoming weaker.

Colonel Nguyen Huy Loi, a veteran staff officer with the JGS and a military adviser to the South Vietnamese delegation to the Paris Talks, thought that Vietnamization had not been approached properly:

> . . . when I was in Paris, people came to ask me, How do you feel about the Vietnamization? I think a Vietnamization program was possible, really, because we did it before, in 1954 with the French. But the important thing is to Vietnamize the whole structure, right from the top, from those who conduct the whole war, not just the small units. . . . We had good officers who would stand and fight but we needed to put them in a right structure of forces.

Q. How would you have Vietnamized?

A. Oh, we talked for a long time in 1966/67 on how the Vietnamese Army had to reorganize in order to become a really effective armed force and to get by alone, with just some support from the U.S. . . . [But] the American forces wanted to train the Vietnamese Army in the image of the American forces. And, as you know, even with American forces we [had not been able to] fight this kind of war. So you have to design some other kind. For a long time I tried to convince our leaders, and I talked with Americans as well, we have to reorganize . . . into *two* forces. One is a territorial force and one is the main force, ready to move anywhere we want. And all these mobile forces have to have adequate support, some ground support . . . I think we needed a large [mobile] force, from ten to fifteen divisions. . . . When I was in Vietnam I made a study of all this . . . [and] tried to submit it to the U.S. and talked to our leaders. And it would have been necessary for the Americans to [withdraw at a slower pace] until we were ready to fight alone. Not just taking the equipment and leave. However, the JGS just stayed there and did nothing. They just did nothing until the end . . . they only received suggestions [from the Americans]. But everything is done at MACV Headquarters and sent to us, that is all.

Q. And you merely translate them and send them . . .

A. Out into the field.

Q. So the JGS didn't do anything?

A. They didn't do anything.

Q. Why?

A. Because everything is done by MACV. And you have the whole system integrated.

Nguyen Ba Can, the man who for a brief period toward the end was Prime Minister after having served for several years as Speaker of the House, reported that:

Vietnamese officials used to call Vietnamization the "U.S. Dollar and Vietnam Blood Sharing Plan." Vietnamization was often

37

praised, but the assistance promised to the Vietnamese, upon which they had come to rely as the key of containment of Communist expansion in South East Asia was denied them after the signing of the Paris Agreements—one might say after the U.S. had staged a "peace with honor" solution.

Continued Complete Reliance on the United States

However, paradoxical though it may seem, feelings of disappointment with the United States, even bitterness, and feelings of having been "abandoned" by the United States because of the Paris Agreements and declining aid apparently went hand in hand with an unshakable conviction that the United States would come to South Vietnam's aid in case of real trouble. Despite their diminishing confidence in U.S. good will or good judgment (as for example in the case of nonresponse to the cease-fire violations, the cease-fire itself, and the declining aid), the leaders, it seems, relied on the United States without reservation. This reliance was based on two factors.

The first of these factors stemmed from the series of face-to-face encounters the Vietnamese had had with American leaders, especially President Nixon, and the written assurances they had received from him. Perhaps the high point in this connection was President Thieu's meeting with President Nixon in San Clemente on April 2–3, 1973—the first (and only) meeting of the two leaders after the traumatic circumstances surrounding the signing of the Paris Agreements. The meeting had pleased the Vietnamese leaders by producing a joint communiqué that threatened "vigorous reaction" to any blatant cease-fire violations by Hanoi.

But Thieu had been even more pleased, according to Bui Diem, who was present at the meeting, with what he was told by President Nixon *privately*. "The off-the-record language was stronger than the language in the official communiqué," stated Diem, "for instance: 'The U.S. will meet all contingencies in case the Agreement is grossly violated,' and, 'You can count on us.'" So pleased and relieved was Thieu with these results of the San Clemente meeting that, again according to Bui Diem, he had champagne broken out to celebrate as soon as his plane was in the air.

Thieu's feeling of being able to rely on the United States in case of serious need was apparently not long affected by the resignation of President Nixon. Bui Diem reported:

> Thieu was visibly shaken at the news of Mr. Nixon's resignation on August 8, 1974, and talked at length with his advisers about the possible repercussions on the Vietnamese situation. His concerns and worries did not last long, however, because just one day later, on August 9 he received from President Ford a letter reassuring him about the continuity of the U.S. policy, a "policy of five presidents," as the letter said. Mr. Thieu displayed the letter in a meeting of the Council of Ministers in Saigon, apparently in an attempt to boost the morale of his entourage and the members of the South Vietnamese government.

If President Ford's letter was fact from which Thieu drew reassurance, he also drew some from fiction. Bui Diem stated:

> This almost total confidence in the continuity and solidity of the U.S. support on the part of Mr. Thieu was reinforced by a lot of rosy reports given to him by many of his advisers who either were over-optimistic or had only a superficial knowledge of American politics. Some of them, like General Dang Van Quang, his well-known Assistant for National Security Affairs, did not want to give bad news to their boss and simply concurred with him whether he praised or blamed the Americans. Others, like the Minister of Planning, Mr. Nguyen Tien Hung, were over-optimistic and gave him incomplete information about the mood in the U.S. I remember in this respect having been really taken by surprise when during a restricted meeting at the Presidental Palace in Saigon [the meeting was convened for an overall assessment of the 1974–1975 U.S. Aid Program to South Vietnam] Mr. Hung reported to President Thieu that according to his own sources, "close to the Pentagon," an amount of 850 millions of dollars was earmarked in the budget of the Pentagon for a possible bombing of North Vietnam. My colleague, Ambassador Tran Kim Phuong from Washington, and I protested against this rather wishful-thinking piece of information, but in these difficult days, perhaps in need of encouragement, Mr. Thieu seemed more inclined to listen to what Mr. Hung reported than to take note of what we said.

An interview with a high-ranking staff officer typified the resulting firm belief down the line in U.S. help in case of true need. This officer was critical of the U.S. failure (he said) to live up to its promise of support to South Vietnam in the event of a major Communist offensive. He had been told that before the GVN had signed the Paris Agreements, President Thieu had received a letter from President Nixon promising a strong U.S. reaction in the event the other side violated the Paris Agreements.

What had helped convince this officer that U.S. air power would come to their aid in case of need was, he stated, the fact that a plan had been worked out by the JGS with the U.S. Defense Attaché's Office outlining the procedures for requesting U.S. air support in the event of a major Communist offensive. He said this plan was never put on paper but resulted from an oral agreement stipulating that President Thieu should formally request U.S. air support through the U.S. Embassy in Saigon, which would then forward the request to the U.S. President. The President in turn would place the request before the U.S. Congress, and it was agreed that South Vietnam had to be prepared to hold on its own for a period of 7 to 15 days until the U.S. procedures could be consummated and a decision on the bombing could be made. This general further stated that hot lines were established between various South Vietnamese commands and the U.S. air base at Nakhon Phanom in Thailand. He said hot-line communications were opened between Nakhon Phanom and the JGS, South Vietnamese Air Force (VNAF) Headquarters in Saigon, and each of the four Corps headquarters, in the event bombing strikes were required. The general also reported that there was a systematic program to update target lists for the U.S. Air Force in Nakhon Phanom.

This staff officer then added that ''every day'' new targeting information was transmitted to the Defense Attaché's Office in Saigon, who in turn passed it on to Nakhon Phanom. Targeting was also updated through periodic visits of senior GVN officers to the air base. The officer said that he flew to Nakhon Phanom three times in 1974 and that General Vien, the Assistant Chief of Staff, Intelligence, and the commanders of I Corps had also made similar base visits. According to him, the agreement concerning target updating, the hot lines, and procedures for requesting air support were put into effect during the first part of 1974. These procedures, he said, were instituted at the initiative of the U.S. Defense Attaché's Office in Saigon, and he assumed that they "must have flowed from an order from a higher echelon" within the United States.

The general stated that he had personally briefed President Thieu on the procedures for requesting U.S. air support in 1974. He added that even though he and others trusted that U.S. air support would be provided in an emergency, efforts to facilitate a positive U.S. decision were not neglected. He said that every Corps commander had received instructions to organize appropriate defense lines and to hold those lines in case of attack so as to make a good impression on the U.S. Congress. He had briefed every Corps commander personally about the procedures for requesting U.S. air support and impressed upon them the necessity of holding, in order to increase the chances of Congressional approval.

Thus most Vietnamese leaders, it seems, including President Thieu himself, expected that the United States would intervene. A man who talked frequently to Thieu during the final months reported:

A. They [the various leaders] believed until 1975 that the Americans would never abandon South Vietnam. A strong feeling from the beginning, all the time.

Q. And in case of outright aggression, we would resume bombing?

A. People didn't pay attention to the mood in the U.S. Congress. . . . They don't know the . . . importance of Congress. They think your Congress is like our Congress. You must understand the psychology of the people. They did not live in America. How could they know how powerful the American Congress is compared with the Vietnamese Congress?

Q. When did this belief [in U.S. intervention] start to erode?

41

A. The last day.

Q. They believed up to the end?

A. That is right.

Q. Do you think Thieu believed that?

A. I think so. . . .

Perceived U.S. Self-Interest

While the first factor underlying Vietnamese expectations of
U.S. help was the apparent belief on the part of the leaders that
they had been promised help in an emergency, the other factor was
their perception of how the United States viewed its own situation
globally. They seemingly were convinced that the United States
could not and would not suffer the conquest of South Vietnam by
the North and its allies for simple reasons of its own self-interest.
In many statements by the Vietnamese respondents, sentences like
the following recurred: "You sacrificed over 50,000 killed in the
war. You had over 200,000 wounded. You spent over 150 billion
dollars. You had at one time over 500,000 men there. You staked
your prestige on a free South Vietnam. How could we ever expect
that you would let South Vietnam go?"[1]

Buu Vien, Assistant Minister of Defense for manpower, briefly
Minister of the Interior, and adviser to Prime Minister Khiem,
summing up what others also said, stated:

> And it was not without sense to reason that way. To begin with, we
> thought the U.S. couldn't afford losing Vietnam because, as a
> superpower, the U.S. would lose face. . . . Second, losing Viet-

[1] Apparently, Air Marshal Nguyen Cao Ky was an exception. He stated, "My
impression is that Thieu always believed that the Americans, because of
worldwide interests, because of strategy, because of this and that, would never let
South Vietnam down, in other words, be occupied by the Communists. . . . I
was the [only one] to repeat and repeat again, even with a map. I told them, look at
Vietnam on the map. Of course, America never wants Vietnam to lose to the
Communists but some day when . . . it's obvious that the Vietnamese cannot
handle the problems themselves, what can Americans do to save us?"

nam would mean that the free world lost the first country to the Communists by war. . . . Third, [if it had not been in the U.S. interest to intervene] the U.S. would not have poured so much resources and sacrificed so many American lives in Vietnam in the first place. The discovery of oil off the Vietnamese coast gave us one more reason to believe the U.S. wouldn't abandon Vietnam. . . . Fourth, the government of South Vietnam had the solid pledge from the U.S. government that the U.S. would react strongly in case of Communist renewed aggression. In the closing session of the San Clemente meeting in 1973 with the Vietnamese delegation, President Nixon made it clear that the U.S. wouldn't let the North Vietnamese Communists take over South Vietnam by force. As Vice Minister of Defense, I was present at the meeting.

And the Vietnamese leaders expected U.S. help not just in the form of air support (B-52s) but also through diplomatic demarches in Moscow or elsewhere.

Finally, the Vietnamese leaders believed that the enemy would reason the same way they did and would therefore desist from waging the type of attack that would precipitate major U.S. military or diplomatic responses. This thought seems to have led them to faulty assessments as to what the enemy would do. Thieu himself is reported to have stated at a meeting in 1974 that the enemy would in all likelihood not make a major attack and would instead resort increasingly to guerrilla warfare and political subversion:

> Even though President Thieu had time and again warned against the possibility of a major Communist final offensive he assumed that political subversion would probably be the main tool the Communists would use to seize control of the country.

From this, it appears that Thieu, too, assumed that the enemy would not want to risk U.S. reactions to a major offensive.[2]

[2] As we are told in the account of the North Vietnamese commander Van Tien Dung, truthfully or not, the Politburo in Hanoi deliberated carefully on the question of whether the United States would respond to a major attack on their part. They eventually concluded that the United States would not. (*Great Spring Victory*, FBIS, Asia and Pacific, APA-76-110, June 7, 1976, p. 5.)

Results of Reliance on U.S. Help

As a result of their conviction that the United States would come to the rescue in case of an emergency, the Vietnamese apparently got the worst of two worlds. On the one hand, they never made any effort to ensure some form of continued national existence through accommodation or negotiation with the other side, social reform, change in leadership, or a coalition government. On the other, relying so unconditionally upon the Americans for help in an emergency, they never "pulled up their socks" to prepare for it. This same attitude later carried over, it seems, into their defense against the final enemy offensive:

> Why fight . . .? They [the Americans] will do something; they will be tough.

The South Vietnamese leaders seem to have reasoned that, without U.S. intervention or sufficient aid, even the most strenuous efforts at self-improvement would be of little value. Hinting that it was foolish of the Americans to expect otherwise, Buu Vien said in his otherwise quite self-critical analysis of the debacle, "No country in contemporary history has been able to prevail against superior military power, no matter what the patriotism of its people or the quality of its government."

This general view, whether it was justified or not, helped to prevent the undertaking of military or civilian reforms—reforms which, in the eyes of a number of the participants/observers, were necessary yet at the same time futile. The only real purpose of undertaking or at least seeming to undertake them appears to have been to propitiate the Americans who, in the minds of South Vietnamese leaders, were impatient, unpredictable, all-powerful, and hard to understand. The only person, they assumed, who knew the Americans and their designs well was Thieu, Saigon's only true connecting point with its ally. It is all the more ironic, then, to learn from one of Thieu's closest confidants (Bui Diem) that the President himself kept asking, "What are the Americans up to?" This was, says Bui Diem, "an obsession in his mind."

In all, the mood in Saigon on the eve of the last big enemy

offensive was one of considerable discouragement caused by the "abandonment" by the Americans—as evidenced, in their view, by the "imposition" of the Paris Agreements, the lack of American response to enemy violations of these Agreements, and declining aid. Yet, at the same time, it was an article of faith with the leaders (and apparently the people, too) that for reasons of self-interest and commitment the United States would never let them fall prey to the North. These feelings of magic invulnerability coupled with profound pessimism about their own capabilities apparently undermined their resistance to such a point that they crumbled more quickly than even the enemy had anticipated. Besides, their blind faith in U.S. help and their conviction that even from a distance the United States remained in control of their destinies lent credence to the rumors that circulated through I Corps in March of 1975 to the effect that a "deal" had been made surrendering northern portions of South Vietnam to the enemy—rumors which apparently contributed greatly to panic and lack of resistance.[3]

[3] This is discussed at length in Part II, in the chapter on the fall of I Corps.

Chapter 2

The Political Situation

The Political Situation

Conflicting Basic Views

Even though South Vietnam's government was, according to Bui Diem, "half a dictatorship," there was, in the view of some respondents, a range of genuine political forces and activities in the country that under more favorable circumstances might have given the people of South Vietnam a working democracy; but when the big enemy push came, their net effect was instead to speed the disintegration of the country through internal opposition.

Underlying some of the manifestations of opposition to Thieu's regime were profound ideological differences, and also some fundamental differences as to what forms any pragmatic approach to the war should take. On the ideological side, statements from some of the respondents indicated that there was disagreement as to whether South Vietnam, in the critical situation created by the war against a powerful and relentless enemy, could "afford" democracy. Some military men, and also Thieu's last Prime Minister, did not think so.[4]

For example, General Nguyen Duy Hinh, the Commander of the 3rd Infantry Division and an officer whose fighting ability was praised by his fellows, stated that there was a need for South Vietnam to fight a "total war" and that national mobilization was imperative. But this, said Hinh, could not be accomplished, given the nature of the free society in South Vietnam. Individuals tended

---

[4] See pp. 56–57.

to pursue their own interests, e.g., seeking higher pay or conducting their own business. In General Hinh's view, democracy was adopted "too early" in South Vietnam and mainly because of American pressure. He cited the criticisms of South Vietnam's authoritarian stance in the U.S. Senate and the way this was used, in his opinion, to justify aid cutbacks.

Hinh also felt that U.S. pressure for village elections in Vietnam was a mistake. He said that the "good people" who would have made desirable candidates in such elections had either migrated to the cities or been killed by the Communists, leaving only "bad people," "draft dodgers," and people "designated" by the Viet Cong infrastructure as candidates for such elections. He considered this "American-fostered village democracy" to be one of the main failures of Pacification. In order to successfully compete with the hard-core Communist organization, it was incumbent on the GVN to set up a counterorganization manned by good cadres. The South needed "regimentation," said Hinh, as well as good leadership both at the presidential and the province chief level. In General Hinh's view, it had therefore been a "mistake" to kill President Diem. Hinh was not sure, however, that even a different system could really have produced a different outcome "because the people had suffered too much, and every family had lost at least one person."

Some other respondents took what seemed to be the opposite view. Rather than thinking that democracy should have been delayed, they felt strongly that extensive social and economic reforms of a democratic nature were needed in order to give the people a cause worth fighting for. The most prominent among the proponents of new political policies was General Tran Van Don, for several years a member of the Senate and a member of a party opposed to Thieu:

> We needed the minds of the people because the problem in Viet-nam was not only military but also social, economic, and political. When I say "political" I don't mean political party, I mean "people". . . . We needed to have a people's army as we have

seen in Israel. [But] we could not ask the people to be involved and to support the struggle, if in this fight we did not change the social order. We [needed] a new social order because what we had was the social order we got from the French side. And it was not a real new social order made by the Vietnamese themselves. The other side, when they opened the war against the South, their motivation was independence and unity and a new social order. We must give the same motivation for the people if you want them to follow you. Independence yes; unity yes; but also a new social order, and we failed to do it.

Beyond such ideological differences between leaders, there were also differences between two forms of pragmatism: Should the armed forces be strengthened at the expense of the economy, or the economy be strengthened at the expense of the armed forces? The leaders, who stated that they were at times subjected to conflicting pressures on this issue by the Americans, vacillated. One general reported that after the Paris Agreements, the GVN was focusing on problems of "post-war reconstruction." National emphasis, particularly after the beginning of 1974, was placed on economic development, with great hopes being pinned on the development of Vietnam's offshore oil resources. In this environment, "everyone neglected the military" and, said the general, the JGS even received an order from President Thieu to demobilize 100,000 men out of the regular forces. The general understood that these men were to be used to help the South Vietnamese increase food production and to satisfy manpower requirements of the civilian ministries. The general added that the JGS had tried to comply with this order and prepared plans for demobilization. However, by the second half of 1974, President Thieu, according to the general, realized that Communist violations of the cease-fire made this plan impractical, and he canceled the order.

There also were disagreements on the crucial questions as to whether or not to seek any kind of accommodation or contact or coalition with the other side. Those who favored the latter course criticized Thieu's so-called policy of the "Four No's": no negotiating with the enemy; no Communist activity in the country;

no coalition government; and no surrender of territory to the enemy. They called him "as inflexible as Diem but with less basic ability." Those who wanted to be more accommodating and flexible wanted to do so primarily on the assumption that there were, in their view, exploitable differences between Hanoi and the Viet Cong, "who had nothing and knew it." Men who wanted to change the political posture of Saigon vis-à-vis the Viet Cong also wanted to "open their hands" to dissenters in Saigon, such as neutralists. None of these ideas of seeking an accommodation with the enemy was ever put into operation until the very end, when in April 1975 "Big Minh" was chosen to negotiate some new arrangement with the other side. But by then it was too late. As Buu Vien put it, "Everything is too late now. The Communists will not accept anything less than unconditional surrender. The rice is already in their mouth. It does not hurt them a bit to chew and swallow it." Such efforts at negotiating, thought Buu Vien (among others), should have come much earlier, right after the conclusion of the Paris Agreements.

Finally, there were differences of opinion among leaders with regard to the political picture in the world at large. One general presented the following reflections on the subject:

President Thieu was probably the man who was most afflicted by the new mood of détente. His staunch anti-Communism seemed to be anachronistic and sometimes bordered on the ridiculous in the new atmosphere of international relaxation of the 70's [the Peking thaw; President Nixon's epochal visits to China and Russia; the tentative rapprochement between North and South Korea; the normalization of relations between East and West Germany]. Furthermore, he created a sort of credibility gap by acting differently from what he professed: as a matter of fact, he preferred not to talk to the Communists, yet he had sent a delegation to Paris; he professed not to make territorial concessions to the Communists, yet he had *de facto* conceded to them all the territory which extended from Thach Han to Ben Hai River and the city of Loc Ninh; he professed never to accept any kind of coalition with the Communists, yet he signed the Paris Agreements which prescribed the creation of the three-party Council for National Concord and

Reconciliation, which was regarded by the Communists as a definite coalition government. Then reversing himself and sticking to his no-coalition policy, he refused to implement this provision, thus providing the Communists with an argument to accuse [the] GVN of bad will and to justify their overt violations of the agreement and their dark intention of annexing the Republic of Vietnam by force.

Since this general considered himself to be very conservative politically, his statements show that even among the conservatives there were serious rifts with regard to how anti-Communist a posture was advisable.

The Mounting Opposition to President Thieu

Partly as the result of such basic differences as outlined above, and partly for reasons of practical politics, the political situation in South Vietnam was felt to have been gradually deteriorating since 1972, so that by the eve of the last great enemy offensive, it had become, in the words of Nguyen Ba Can, "political chaos."

According to Can, most political forces in the country had turned away from President Thieu in the predisaster period of 1974. These political forces had not always been unable to rise above partisan concerns in times of emergency. They had done just that, according to Can, in 1968 and 1972, during the two big enemy offensives, when despite their lack of sympathy for Thieu they had thrown their support behind him and the war effort. But, according to Can, "in 1975 most people not only failed to support the government, they opposed it—strongly."

There was, said Can, not only "political chaos" in Saigon in 1974 and early 1975 but, in fact, "anarchy." For one thing, Thieu had lost the support of the Catholics who had been his staunchest anti-Communist allies. Can attributed this to a shift in Vatican policy in favor of "accommodation," which according to Can, the Pope had recommended to a disappointed Thieu when they had met in 1973 and to an obedient Catholic hierarchy in South Vietnam. Presumably, the Vatican had concluded already that the cause of South Vietnam was lost and, as Thieu observed to Can, "had begun to lean toward a policy that would perhaps make life easier for Catholics behind the Iron Curtain."

However, some Catholics went much further than merely failing to support the Thieu government. In mid-1974, Father Tran Huu Thanh's "anti-corruption movement" that was backed initially by only a dozen out of some three thousand priests living in South Vietnam had, according to Can, as its unnamed, though obvious, target the President himself. The campaign snowballed into a major political force in the country and carried with it the switch of Catholics in the Assembly from a friendly to a hostile posture. This occurred, said Can, at a "strange time," because Thieu had finally just purged the armed forces of many corrupt officers. While he thereby incurred the anger of the armed forces he failed to diminish the fervor of the anti-corruption campaign.

This turning away of the Catholics was called by Can "the most catastrophic political move." He added:

> The Vietnamese Catholic community, which was the best organized [force] in the country fighting Communism, now [in 1974] abandoned its will to resist and took steps toward coexistence.

At the same time, the Hoa Hao in the Mekong Delta, who had supported the government, changed their stance toward the Thieu regime. Their new opposition was expressed by their practice of not only giving refuge and protection to hundreds of thousands of deserters from ARVN and the draft, but also organizing them into a force of their own and arming them with American weapons purchased from corrupt ARVN officers. Having formed what they called a "Civil Guard Force," the Hoa Hao became a formidable adversary for Thieu, who was faced with the dilemma of either letting them be or openly fighting them. Thieu chose the latter course at great cost to himself.

The An Quang Buddhists, who had long been a problem to the authorities in Saigon, also increased their resistance in 1974-1975. They created a variety of movements "with clandestine Communist leanings and connections; fomented street disorder in Saigon; and, in cooperation with Buddhist congressmen, once

54

even seized the Lower House and covered it with anti-government slogans.''

Finally, according to Hantho Touneh, a prominent Montagnard who served as Secretary General in the Ministry for the Development of Ethnic Minorities in Saigon, the Saigon government now was presented the bill for having seriously alienated the Montagnards in the highlands over the years through a policy of ruthless exploitation of their territories and suppression of their people. Touneh reported:

> When I was [in my post] I received many reports from the Ethnic Minority Services . . . which mentioned many incidents in the Montagnard areas (between Vietnamese and Montagnards). . . . The Vietnamese soldiers came to the villages and stole the chickens and killed the animals, destroyed crops, burned houses and arrested . . . villagers. . . .

He further stated:

> The Montagnards believed in the military strength of the government [Saigon] but were disappointed with many high-ranking ARVN officers who supported Vietnamese contractors to exploit the lumber in the Montagnards' areas. . . .

and

> It was also reported to me that the Montagnard soldiers were treated unjustly . . . whenever there was a question of promotion, it was always given to the Vietnamese and denied to the Montagnard soldier.

Thus, a catalog of grievances against the Saigon regime had eventually accumulated among the Montagnards, too.

Thieu's Reaction

When Thieu was faced with all this opposition, the power base on which he had operated over the years after using Prime Minister (and General) Khiem to deprive Air Marshal Ky of most of the

55

latter's effective power, began to erode rather rapidly. Thieu's situation became even more precarious when he allegedly had a falling out with Khiem over his efforts to retain the presidency for a third term.

When Khiem managed to have most of Thieu's special assistants transferred to a newly formed Cabinet (which he headed) in early 1975, a situation arose which was described as follows by Nguyen Ba Can:

> With his presidential office and the party dismantled, Thieu was reduced to impotence. He spent his time playing tennis and water-skiing on the Saigon River more often than at any other time, while the security situation was deteriorating and becoming worse than it had ever been before. And the people were disoriented by so much internal trouble happening all of a sudden.
>
> In the meantime, either because of a fatal combination of circumstances or as a result of some magical orchestration, the religious and political parties, the press and other influential groups such as the lawyers—even those traditionally regarded as favorable to the government—expressed their discontent and seemed united in a front of protest which brought disorder to the country, thus affecting seriously the armed forces' morale and the population's confidence.

As a result of the many political pressures and the endless strains of the war, the country was, at the time of the big attacks, on the verge of a "psychological collapse that struck every South Vietnamese, be he top leader or regular citizen, military or civilian, commander or private soldier," and led to Thieu's "inconceivable strategic mistakes, the panicky mass exodus from the cities, and ARVN's total collapse."

Can added, "It is important to consider that there were two categories of people in Vietnam. One category had to fight for the other category—I mean the armed forces. Only the armed forces had the responsibility to fight the war, in the opinion of the people. The people remained outside of this. They were not involved in the fight. It was the opposite of a 'people's war.' The way we conducted war, we should have realized that in the long run we had to

56

lose it." Can, like some other respondents, stated, "Even the political concepts of the regime were not suitable for such a war. There was modern democracy. There was disorder, chaos. We would have needed a strong power. We needed more discipline, to get the people involved. To get all the people to fight for themselves."

The political situation on the eve of the final enemy offensive was summarized by Can, who was one of the most knowledgeable respondents on the subject of political affairs in South Vietnam, having held high office for many years. He said:

> Sooner or later, South Vietnam had to fall into Communist hands. That had been expected by those who had followed closely the development of the endless war in that area of the world. This was expected by the leaders of the Republic of Vietnam too. But what astonished all of them was the sudden collapse of the nation that had one of the most powerful [armed] forces in Asia and that demonstrated its determination to fight regardless of the price it had to pay. . . .

and concluded:

> To sum up, the war was lost from its inception.

These words are significant, not only for the assessment they express (which may or may not be correct) but also because they reflect the profound pessimism of some of the men in leading positions in South Vietnam.

Chapter 3

The Leadership

The Leadership

Thieu

When talking about the leadership in South Vietnam before the collapse, we are talking basically about President Thieu. Thieu's was—or appeared to be—a one-man rule, or what would be called a dictatorship. But, from what the respondents report, the man was nevertheless *sui generis*, and so was his regime.

According to Bui Diem:

> It used to be said in Saigon as a joke that South Vietnam was a country with half of everything. It was half democracy and half dictatorship, and the measures taken by the government were most of the time half-measures. The result of this was that nothing worked as it should.

In a more serious vein, Diem continued:

> A one-man regime is usually a strong and efficient regime. Quite the contrary was the case in Vietnam. The President had all the power in his hands and could easily impose his policy, but somehow there was no sense of purpose or direction among the high officials of the government and *strangely enough, in a country so pressed by the requirements of war, not a single member of the government, including the President himself, had any sense of urgency about the situation. . . .*[5]

[5] Emphasis added by the authors.

What were the origins of this man, and how was he looked upon by other leaders in South Vietnam? One general, who was, among other positions in his career, the Commandant of the Military Academy in Dalat, said:

> President Thieu was a good officer but he was a mediocre general. His combat record was unimpressive. He was born in the Province of Ninh Thuan (Phan Rang), south of Cam Ranh Bay, of middle-class parents. His character and moral values were strongly influenced by the hard life in his native village where the lands are poor and rocky, and where it rains during only one month of the year. People there must struggle without respite against nature to extract enough to eat from the recalcitrant soil and from the sterile sea. Young Thieu left his village to try his fortunes in the French Colonial Army until the time he enrolled in the officers school in Hue. In 1948 he became an officer in the Vietnamese Army. Thieu was very suspicious by nature and would not hesitate to fight viciously to attain success in life. He was also very patient and able to wait for a long time, and he waited until the self-destruction of his opponents was complete and he could come to power without competition.

In all, the respondents had very few good things to say about Thieu, and a great deal that was unfavorable. Even though some respondents gave Thieu high marks as a military commander, others stated that he was inept as a political and military leader; that he appointed incompetent and corrupt men to high military positions; that he had a virtual passion for inaction; that his leadership was impaired by the fact that he trusted nobody and was not trusted by anybody; and that he was involved in the extensive corruption plaguing the country. Moreover, his appointments of others to high office, both military and civilian, had no admirers, even among the men who participated in this study (and who owed their own positions to Thieu). According to one general:

> Thieu was a man of conflicting personality. He trusted no one and if he had a few confidants whom he sometimes listened to, they were

all corrupt, and arrogant. This conflicting personality was reflected in the field of strategy. We may say that as far as national strategy is concerned, we had no strategy at all, or rather we had a conflicting strategy. For instance, President Thieu first ordered his field commanders to defend everything, to defend every inch of terrain, even the smallest and most remote town; then he decided, after the fall of Ban Me Thuot, to surrender too many things. It is true that we could not have an independent strategy as long as we had to rely too much on foreign aid, but the lack of a coherent military strategy was due most of all to the ineptitude of our military leaders and the lack of a good planning organization. . . . The National Security Committee was headed by General Dang Van ("Fat") Quang, Special Assistant for Military and Security Affairs, the most corrupt and the most hated man in Vietnam, who spent all of his time [looking] for a better way of making money instead of planning a sound and coherent strategy for the country.

Allegedly, most of Thieu's thinking was aimed at staying in power. This required two things above all, neither of them very conducive to good governing: (1) He had to avoid becoming the victim of a new coup, and (2) he had to continue to have the exclusive support of the Americans:

President Thieu had in his mind all the time the fear of a coup against himself, and he was very happy to have General Cao Van Vien, a very quiet man, a not very exciting man, to be chief of staff. And Thieu also liked not to see close cooperation between the General Staff and the four Corps Headquarters. . . . He was all the time afraid of a government by the generals. (He did not even want them to meet with each other.) He had in mind that if all these people [got] together to talk about the military situation, they would also discuss the political situation and make a coup.

General Tran Van Don, lapsing into French, described Thieu also as "méchant," a word that has a meaning somewhere between nasty and evil. Don, who stated that Thieu "didn't like me very much," further characterized Thieu as follows:

63

Every move he made was to consolidate his position with the Americans, or at least not put it in danger. He never trusted anybody in his entourage or in the armed forces; this had a corroding effect. Yet, he did not trust the Americans either, despite their support. He was scared every day that he would lose their support, and therefore was no more comfortable with them than he was with his compatriots. He was very intelligent, but used that intelligence mainly to [cement] his position. He was also corrupt.

Most portraits drawn of Thieu by other South Vietnamese leaders, aside from being generally uncomplimentary with regard to Thieu's leadership ability and personal integrity, converge on his having been given—almost dedicated—to *inaction*. [6] In fact, it is possible that, aside from being a personal proclivity on the part of Thieu, inaction may have been a deliberate policy on his part to alleviate possible U.S. apprehensions concerning rash actions. In any event, Thieu's basic military and political policies were all encompassed by his "Four No's," which he promulgated after the Paris Agreements. These were indeed guides to inaction rather than action. Not unlike the Roman General Fabius Maximus Cunctator who obtained his byname "Cunctator" (the hesitator) by refusing to give Hannibal battle until the latter defeated himself through unwise moves, Thieu apparently believed that the policy of waiting out his opponents, which had worked so well for him personally on his way to the top, might also work in the war.

Thieu apparently also was very slow to change his mind. One former staff officer reported that aside from the fact that Thieu stubbornly clung to ideas and policies once he had developed them, nothing was gained even if someone could convince him that a certain policy might be wrong. In such cases, said the officer, Thieu still refused to act in alternate fashion, saying, "All right, perhaps the current policy is wrong. But how can I be sure

[6] This is in striking contrast to Nguyen Cao Ky, a flamboyant activist, nicknamed by some of his fellow officers "the cowboy," who was always trying to "go North," or imploring General Vien to let him counterattack at Ban Me Thuot at the head of a tank column, or hoping to transform Saigon "into a Stalingrad." In his own interview, when asked to assess the probability of the success of such undertakings, Ky would say, "You don't know unless you try."

that the new policy you suggest will not also prove to be wrong?'' Another witness of high military rank and responsibility reported that Thieu was extremely difficult to talk to because ''he was joking all the time.'' This appears to be yet more evidence that Thieu had his own ways of evading demands for action.

Although Thieu was extremely suspicious by nature, he seems to have been at the same time quite naive or gullible on occasion. An example concerns the discovery of offshore oil. As described by Buu Vien:

> Most dramatic . . . was the discovery of oil off the Vietnamese coast. . . . I recall a meeting at which the oil news was announced by the Minister of Economy. President Thieu, in a jubilant mood, nodded to me, saying, ''Regarding the new cars ordered for the coming state visits, let's now buy ten of them instead of two.'' He went on to remark jokingly, ''Maybe in the future all we need in our government will be a President and one minister of oil.'' For all those present at the meeting (including Thieu), it seemed that the discovery of oil might hold the magic power to solve all the country's economic problems, and for a moment it seemed that the news had dissipated all their worries.

Apparently, Thieu was also very slow in establishing relations with individual Americans. Bui Diem reported that Ambassador Martin once told him, ''I want to help your country and your President, but the only thing your President has asked me to do until now is to make arrangements for your Vice-President to go to Washington to Walter Reed Hospital for a checkup.'' When Bui Diem queried Thieu about this, he was told, ''I do not know him [Martin] well yet, so I have to go slow in my relations with him.'' This, said Bui Diem, ''was a situation in which the relations between the two allies were outwardly correct but not at all normal, considering the fact that the war obviously required a closer coordination. This situation lasted until the final days of the war.''

One observer stated, ''Thieu was suspicious of all personalities who showed any potential to replace him as President. This was true in particular with regard to Prime Minister Khiem. Thieu [believed] that Khiem would be his rival in the next presidential election.''

Allegedly, Thieu's distrust of those around him had adverse consequences on the conduct of government business. One respondent who at times attended Council of Ministers meetings related, "In order to avoid arousing any further suspicions in Thieu, Prime Minister Khiem chose to be quiet. He hardly ever expressed his views in the Council of Ministers meeting. He confided to me that it did not serve any purpose to argue with the President in the presence of his ministers. Anything he found important to convey to him he would say privately to the President. This discreet attitude might have saved Khiem trouble with Thieu, but it also contributed to the confusion of the leadership and sometimes caused regrettable delays in the implementation of government programs. Ministers became confused. . . ." In fact, according to the same source, conversations with Thieu at the meetings were so guarded and Thieu's own statements so vague that on many occasions long meetings were held by the ministerial council just for the purpose of interpreting what Thieu might have meant by what he said.

As for Thieu's proclivity to interfere personally in military operations, bypassing the JGS and dealing directly with the Corps commanders, one witness reported that Thieu did this not wholly for reasons of personal expediency: "Being an Army general, the President actually enjoyed the idea of personally exercising his authority as the Commander-in-Chief of the armed forces, and he could not resist the temptation to direct military operations from his office. . . . Meanwhile the Ministry of Defense had no real authority over the JGS (which itself had little authority). . . . During my three years in the government, I had occasion to observe that the President seemed to want to decide on everything himself. He was reluctant to share the heavy national burden with other members of the government, causing the latter to evade their own responsibilities; and when the President failed to act, nearly everything came to a standstill." Clearly, these traits and this style of governing became even more pronounced during the great crisis of 1975.

One aspect of Thieu's leadership seems to have changed drastically over time: Whereas in earlier days his orders to military leaders, according to several of them, had been very "precise,"[7] they later became increasingly Delphic. This may also have had something to do with the fact that, according to General Tran Van Don, Thieu as a man and leader had been in decline for several years:

A. I said to Thieu many times to regroup the Regional Forces. But I feel that in 1974 Thieu had decreased capability.

Q. He became tired?

A. Not tired; physically he was in good shape. But he seemed not to believe, and I was not sure that he [wanted] to be reelected in 1975. The summer of 1972 he was on top of his power. . . . He was on top in 1972 and 1973. After that he was decreasing.

According to one staff officer whose opinions differ from those of most of the other witnesses, Thieu deserves credit for some good judgment, even though Thieu had ruled against him when he and the Corps commanders had recommended that remote outposts be abandoned and the forces defending them be regrouped.

According to this staff officer, Thieu's reasoning was that the maintenance of the outposts was necessary to assure South Vietnamese control of the countryside surrounding them and, further, it was necessary for South Vietnam to insist that the Paris Agreements be respected on all counts. When asked how he reacted to President Thieu's rejection of this military advice from his senior officers, this respondent said that Thieu was "Commander-in-Chief" and a "general who knows his business." He stated that Thieu probably had his own political purposes in refusing to give up the outposts at any cost and speculated that the president may

[7] Some sources opined that one reason for Thieu's giving orders personally after the Paris Agreements was that there was then a distinct political component to every military move.

have been trying therewith to prove Communist violations of the cease-fire.

Tran Van Don—no friend of Thieu's—also gave him credit for "intelligence" in the following revealing narrative:

> In 1974 Thieu called [a well-known astrologer to the palace] and presented him one question: "If I resign . . . can you with your astrology see who is capable to replace me, including Big Minh?" [The astrologer] said to Thieu, "I don't see anyone, including Big Minh, to take your place if you resign." And you know how Thieu reacted? Very intelligent. He is a very intelligent man. He was with me when I commanded I Corps. He was not too intelligent when he was one of my division commanders. But he was more intelligent when he became president. And Thieu said, "If nobody can replace me, that means I will be replaced by the Communists. . . ."

Ky, who is one of Thieu's bitterest critics, saw the solution to what some observers regard as the Thieu riddle in one single, simple answer which does Thieu little honor: Thieu expected from the beginning that things would not work out in Vietnam and that he eventually would have to flee the country. Thieu, according to Ky, prepared for his departure from Vietnam "all along." Thieu's readiness to leave the country, said Ky, was known to or at least sensed by other generals and had a devastating effect on them in 1975:

A. At that time (early 1975) Thieu was preparing to go.

Q. Thieu was preparing to go? To leave the country?

A. Yes, and some top generals too, ready to go.

Q. This was before Danang fell? They were preparing to leave already?

A. Yes.

Q. What were they doing? Were they packing suitcases? How does one know they were preparing to leave? What physical evidence? Did you talk to their wives, servants, how do you know?

A. Actually, Thieu prepared his retreat years ago. . . . I know Thieu very well, and he knew the military situation.

Strangely enough, Thieu, despite the solid support he received over the years from the Americans, was, according to some witnesses, constantly worried about that support even though (or maybe because) he often procrastinated in fulfilling his promises to the U.S. Ambassador. Ky went further than most in his description of Thieu's insecurity on the score of American support:

Q. . . . apparently [Thieu] always worried about the support of the Americans. . . . Even though he had all the support he still worried about it?

A. Oh, always. I remember when I was head of the Vietnamese delegation in [the] Paris talks, every time I came back and told him about the developments and of course, all the problems, every time I discussed with him, the first question he asked me is, "What [do the] Americans think?" He always was worried about that. He even said, "Well, you know, they may kill me any time if I do something against them." He was always scared about what would happen.

Q. About being assassinated?

A. He was always worried about that.

Q. He was serious about that? That was his serious fear?

A. Oh, very serious. . . .

And in the end, says Ky, Thieu slept every night in a different room in order to evade assassination attempts.

The fear of being killed by the Americans, or perhaps by others with American consent, was ascribed to Thieu by General Tran Van Don as well. Don said that Thieu was not so much afraid of a "soft" coup as he was of what he called a "hard" coup in which he would lose his life. This, according to some, was the reason Thieu recalled the Airborne Division from I Corps at the time of the fall of Ban Me Thuot. This is a matter of controversy among respondents, however; some agree that fear for his life was indeed

69

Thieu's motive, others do not. If it is correct that Thieu withdrew the Airborne Division primarily for the purpose of protecting his own life, in view of the disastrous effects this withdrawal is said by most respondents to have had in I Corps, he took a step that he must have known would or at least could endanger the defense of the entire country.

One observer concluded his observations on Thieu as follows:

> If anyone is to be blamed for the fall of South Vietnam, the Vietnamese military leaders were primarily responsible. It was they who brought Thieu to power. When it became clear that Thieu failed the Vietnamese cause, they and they alone had the responsibility and the capability to dismiss him. Unfortunately for the Vietnamese people, they failed to do so.

Other South Vietnamese Leaders

As for other aspects of the leadership in South Vietnam, the respondents' comments were mostly negative. They spoke of incompetent generals who were "improvisers" who had not acquired the fundamentals of the military arts in the appropriate colleges; of scheming and rapacious wives of high military and civilian officials who wielded vast power over goods and people; of cowardly commanders who avoided enemy action; of blatantly corrupt military and civilian leaders in Saigon and in the provinces. And to single out one individual who for many observers symbolized all that was wrong with the leadership in Saigon, the respondents pointed frequently to General Dang Van Quang, contemptuously referred to as "Fat Quang," a man who was said to have had huge black market dealings in rice, the people's main food, and in opium as well, and who as *éminence grise* (or one might say *noire)* behind Thieu's chair apparently enjoyed a close relationship with the President and wielded enormous power. Such leaders, according to some of the witnesses, had little concern for the people, and the people had little respect for them.

This popular disrespect was aggravated by the fact that most of the leaders had had overly close connections with the Americans.

One general said that in times of extreme national emergency it should be possible to sacrifice some national sovereignty (he saw the American presence in Vietnam as such a sacrifice of some sovereignty), but that this sacrifice was creating political and ultimately military hazards in Vietnam:

> Since the dependence and subordination of the Vietnam government was so obviously demonstrated by the predominant presence and power of the Americans, the Vietnamese general public could not refrain from viewing their government as a puppet deprived of all national prestige, lacking in national mandate and thus being untrustworthy. In [such] a highly ideological struggle as the Vietnam war, this aspect had a strong negative impact and worked much to the detriment of the RVN cause. Moreover, reacting to the negative attitude of the Vietnam public, RVN officials were unwilling or afraid to take any initiative and were thus reduced to adopting a defensive attitude.

This long list of negative statements made by former South Vietnamese leaders about their own leadership was punctuated only rarely by positive statements about anyone, military or civilian, although some senior commanders were praised. The late Ngo Dinh Diem was described by several observers as a good national leader—better, in their view, than anyone who followed. And quite a few positive statements of a general nature were made about lower grade officers. But that just about exhausts the meager list of favorable comments any of the respondents had for anyone in the leadership structure.

Some of the respondents, in fact, opined that the poor quality of their leadership, as they saw it, was doubly pernicious in a poor country with new institutions. One general prefaced his observations on leadership as follows:

> In a poor country, torn and divided by a long war, the leadership is [especially] important.

Others expressed similar views, pointing to what they considered to be the difference between the United States, where the effective functioning of a well-established system was less dependent on the personalities of the leaders, and South Vietnam, where personalities were of paramount importance.

Passivity in Leadership

A number of the respondents complained that passivity had become ingrained in South Vietnam's leadership. The inherent power and omnipresence of the United States, coupled with South Vietnam's situation of total dependency, reduced South Vietnam's own leaders to submissive order takers. One high-ranking general asserted that the Americans guaranteed this by insuring the selection of Vietnamese who were willing to be cooperative.

According to Tran Van Don, General Vien recognized the subservient role of the South Vietnamese. Another general officer agreed that South Vietnam's leaders had been reduced to carrying out American plans, and he provided an example: "When I was division commander and a Corps commander, every year I got a heavy book and it was the military plan. And when I read the plan, on one side is Vietnamese and on the other is English. And I see that it is translated from the English and is not the plan of General Vien. So I think this is no good because General Vien didn't do anything—he let General Westmoreland's staff write the plan and they sent a copy of the plan to General Vien and J3 translated it into Vietnamese and signed."

Buu Vien noted that pleasing the Americans became the principal goal of South Vietnam's officers:

> The presence of American advisers at all levels of the military hierarchy created among the Vietnamese leadership a mentality of reliance on their advice and suggestions. Even though some officers didn't like the intrusive presence of their American counterparts, most of them felt more confident when they had their advisers at their sides. The ideas might be theirs, but they felt more assured when those ideas were concurred in by American advisers than when they were suggested by their superiors. Officers talking about their performance never failed to mention how much they were being appreciated by their American counterparts as though

appreciation by American advisers was evidence of their success, their command ability, their honesty.

This feeling extended to the highest levels of South Vietnam's government. As Bui Diem observed, President Thieu "always considered the American factor the most important element—if not the vital one—in every problem that he had to solve, whether it was concerning the future of the country or his own political future." Colonel Nguyen Huy Loi supported this observation: "I think that in Thieu's mind the Americans were responsible for everything and they [the South Vietnamese leaders] didn't need to do anything. And everyone just sit down and wait because they think the Americans are responsible for everything." Most South Vietnamese would have agreed with Thieu, for in their eyes his selection as president was itself an American decision.[8]

These sentiments were echoed by Air Marshal Ky, who complained about South Vietnam's loss of identity: ". . . most of the time, because [of] your role, because [of] your responsibilities, [the] Americans were playing a dominant role, and at the end we lost our own identity."

Colonel Vu Van Uoc, the Chief Operations Officer of the South Vietnamese Air Force (VNAF), also stated:

> . . . during the years 1964-72 when U.S. troops were actively fighting in South Vietnam, most campaigns and big military opera-

[8] It should be noted that many of the observations made by senior South Vietnamese officials after the collapse closely parallel those made by the younger officers, mostly of the post-1954 generation, who were interviewed in Saigon in 1971. At that time, these younger officers pointed out that many officers of the older generation had served as NCOs in the French Army. As a result, said the younger officers, they had developed French tastes and a *mentalité de colonisé* and would still be saluting French officers if the French Army were still in Vietnam. The younger officers derogatorily referred to the older soldiers as *Saigon Parisiens*. Sometimes they used a more powerful Vietnamese word, *no boc*, which means lackey or slave, as the people conquered by the Vietnamese in the past were called *no boc*. These former French NCOs now took their orders from a new set of foreigners, Americans, whose views they reflected. The young officers felt that the South Vietnamese Army which was being built up with American assistance and American guidance was merely an extension of the American Army, which had not succeeded in Vietnam.

73

tions were placed under American supervision. Even in joint U.S./Vietnamese operations, ARVN was only given a minor role and air force tactics were placed under the supervision of American advisers. In that situation, ARVN felt a too-heavy dependence upon U.S. forces and one can hardly say these operations were under Vietnamese jurisdiction. The same policy was applied to high-ranking and also to combat officers, so that ARVN completely lost the notion of being an independent army.

Corruption and Leadership

A central feature of the South Vietnamese regime, according to most respondents, was corruption. It would serve no purpose in this overview to render all the details about trade in foodstuffs and drugs; about "cinnamon generals" who used division-size forces to trade in their favorite commodity; about officers who supported concubines on a grand scale with ill-gotten gains; about rackets reaching into the highest quarters of government, including the Presidential Palace; or about the ubiquitous wives of prominent men who had their bejeweled fingers in every lucrative pie and were highly skilled in giving bribes, receiving payoffs, and obtaining posts for their husbands. These stories have received ample news coverage; from what some of the respondents said, it would appear that many of them were true.

Rather, the essential *effects* of corruption, as seen by the respondents, will be summarized here in a few sentences. In the first place, there was not one high-ranking person in the Saigon government who was not accused by at least some of the respondents as having participated in the corruption and profited from it. Second, corruption principally took one of four forms: racketeering in scarce and often vital goods; bribery of officials; buying and selling of big jobs and appointments; and—last but by no means least—the collection of army pay from "ghost soldiers" and "roll-call soldiers." As to the last technique, the method was simple. Soldiers who had been killed or who had deserted were not taken off the payroll, and their salaries were pocketed by their superiors. Similarly, "roll-call" soldiers, who actually existed but

74

appeared only for roll call, would yield their salary to their superiors in return for being permitted to be absent from duty. Considering that casualties throughout the entire war were very heavy and an estimated 100,000 soldiers deserted annually, it is clear that the sums collected on a regular basis by those who participated in the "ghost soldiers" schemes were enormous.

A further result of carrying so many "ghost soldiers" on the rolls was that many units that were severely understrength did not reveal themselves as such until caught in combat.

One crippling effect of such corruption, according to the witnesses, was that it permitted men to obtain offices for which they were not qualified, particularly military commands. Another was that corruption destroyed morale.

"Clans existed from the lower to the higher rank; the majority of the high-ranking commanders were servants to the Thieu regime and they brought up a number of lazy, corrupted and unqualified generals for their servile obedience . . . so destroying the fighting morale of the young ARVN officers." The Montagnard leader Hantho Touneh attributed the erosion of leadership in the Ministry for the Development of Ethnic Minorities to the corruption of the Thieu administration. And finally, said Colonel Nguyen Huy Loi, the cutbacks in American aid that reduced the flow of personal profits to the Vietnamese leaders affected their motivation to fight in 1975. From their point of view, it made more sense "to take your winnings and run." In other words, if we can believe Loi, to benefit from corruption was actually the principal motivation of a substantial part of the military and civilian leadership.

But the effects of the all-pervading corruption, according to the respondents, went even deeper than that. One commander said:

> Corruption always engenders social injustice. In Vietnam, a country at war, social injustice was more striking than in any other country. Corruption had created a small elite which held all the power and wealth, and a majority of middle-class people and peasants who became poorer and poorer and who suffered all the sacrifices. It was these people who paid the taxes to the government, the bribes to the police, who had to buy fertilizer at exorbi-

tant prices and to sell their rice at a price fixed by the government, and it was also these people who sent their sons to fight and die for the country while high government officials and wealthy people sent theirs abroad. An army doctor once told me that he was disheartened to see that all the wounded, all the amputees who crowded his hospital came from the lower class, from the peasants' families, and that they had suffered and sacrificed for a small class of corrupt elite. The government professed to win the heart and the mind of the people, but all it had done was to create a widening gap between the leadership and the mass; and this increasing conflict, this internal contradiction, if we were to use Communist parlance, could not last; it had somehow to be resolved. Unfortunately it was resolved in the Communist way.

From this and similar statements, it would appear that corruption was considerably more than a problem that could have been solved by the firing of a few generals and civilians. It was regarded by many of the respondents as a fundamental ill that was largely responsible for the ultimate collapse of South Vietnam. As with other grave defects of the system, the respondents did not, on the whole, present measures that could have remedied the situation. They did, however, politely hint on occasion that, in their view, with Thieu involved in the corruption, there was no way of curbing it as long as the Americans supported him in office.

In sum, according to the respondents, who often roundly and acerbically denounced the very leadership of which they had themselves been part, the leadership in South Vietnam encompassed all the worst possible features: It was authoritarian without having true authority. It was military without being competent or innovative in military affairs. It was a form of one-man rule without the leader being a popular man.[9] The government was corrupt, inefficient, and regarded by the people to some extent as a puppet of the Americans. It was nonfunctioning at the top and, as some claimed, had no dedicated cadre at the middle levels. And in the most urgent situation, it had no sense of urgency.

[9] On the subject of "popularity," respondents did not seem to share the widespread American view that at least "Big Minh" was popular. "Perhaps as a tennis partner for Maxwell Taylor," said one general with a laugh. Where, then, did Minh's reputation come from? "From the United States! *You* built him up!"

Chapter 4

U.S.-Vietnamese Relations

U.S.-Vietnamese Relations

There is no aspect to the war in Vietnam—or to any subject discussed in this report—that is not in some way connected with U.S.-Vietnamese relations. Vietnamese politics, strategies, force posture, hopes, and expectations—these were all part of and permeated with what the Americans did or wanted, and what the Vietnamese thought the Americans did or wanted.

In general, most respondents seemed to feel that the alliance relationship with the Americans was not a success. They placed a good deal, but by no means all, of the blame for this upon American shoulders. They accepted some of the burden for the failures, but they seemed to leave open the question of whether such cooperation could, in fact, have been more fruitful.

One respondent, Bui Diem, said:

> The South Vietnamese understood neither American policies nor American politics, and in my personal opinion one of the tragedies of the Vietnam War was the fact that due rather to an unexpected happening of international circumstances, two peoples quite apart in terms of civilization, mentality, international status and geographic position were thrown together in a war against a common enemy when Americans understood very little about Vietnam and Vietnamese knew nothing about America . . . the few things that the Vietnamese knew about the U.S. were the generous Marshall Plan, the strong anti-Communist and moralistic stand of John Foster Dulles, and the idealistic inaugural address by John Kennedy. For them the U.S. involvement in Vietnam was but a logical

continuation of Korea. . . . The Vietnamese faith in the U.S. was reinforced by the presence of more than half a million GIs, and no one could believe that the U.S. might give up only a few years later.

Personal proximity apparently did not always enhance understanding:

In the eyes of the South Vietnamese, the Americans created for themselves extra difficulties by making the war too expensive by the way they fought it. The men from the "affluent society" brought into Vietnam a new kind of war never seen or even thought of before. The Vietnamese opened their eyes wide in bewilderment when they saw U.S. forces supplied with hot meals by helicopter while still in combat. They saw the thousands of unnecessary gadgets piled high in huge PXs, the hundreds of planes crossing the Pacific for the transport of American troops on rotation. They witnessed the more than generous use of bombs and ammunition by the U.S. forces, and hours of bombing and strafing . . . triggered in many instances by mere sniper fire. They said among themselves, especially when [in 1974] the Congress rejected their request for more military aid, that the critics in the U.S. were really unfair in putting responsibility for all these billions consumed by the war on their shoulders; and that if the Americans could only have saved part of the cost of just a few weeks of their stay in Vietnam and used the saving for aid, the outcome could perhaps [have been] different.

Diem added:

For the man in the street, for those who had nothing to do with politics and had no vested interest for or against the government in Saigon, the way of reasoning was more down-to-earth, though based on a lot of common sense. In their eyes, the U.S. somehow forced its way into South Vietnam by sending hundreds of thousands of troops into the country, and should therefore bear the consequences of this decision, whether it was good or bad. A big nation and world power like the U.S. should show some sort of responsible behavior or at least a moral obligation to help the South

80

Vietnamese out of a situation that precisely the presence of the U.S. troops had contributed to create. The Americans should and could not simply call it quits after putting the whole house of Vietnam in shambles and say, for instance: "That is enough for us, we now have our own problems at home; besides we have discovered that the involvement stemmed from the wrong decision." . . . It was within this context and in this environment that Mr. Thieu . . . shaped his own perceptions of U.S. policy. As a Vietnamese and military man he shared many of the ideas held by his countrymen. But as a cautious politician and complex man he had rather complicated ideas about the U.S. policy. Basically, he did not trust the Americans. But at the same time he was convinced, deep in his heart, that the Americans would never give up in Vietnam. One might wonder . . . how Mr. Thieu, so suspicious by nature, did not have questions in his mind about the solidity of the U.S. support and why a man whose constant question was ''What are the Americans up to?'' could fail to take into consideration the possibility of an American pull-out.

Diem explained the seeming riddle in this way:

An explanation is given by Mr. Hoang Duc Nha, cousin of Mr. Thieu and one of his closest aides . . .: Mr. Thieu was suspicious of the Americans *only as far as his own political future was concerned.* During times of crisis . . . his suspicion was centered on the possibility of an American sponsored coup *against him personally,* but basically he held the belief that the Americans would never tolerate a takeover of South Vietnam by the Communists, at least not in the foreseeable future. . . .

In a way, several threads seem to come together here. Thieu, as indicated earlier, regarded a major Communist offensive or a vigorous Communist infiltration followed by an eventual takeover as possible. According to witnesses, his conclusion was that the Communists would choose the latter route. It may well be that this faulty conclusion, which must have greatly affected his conduct of civilian and military affairs, was based on his assumption that even though the enemy might be tempted to mount a major attack, the

81

Americans would not tolerate it. Thus the enemy would probably select instead a policy of massive subversion and infiltration which would be harder to treat as an obvious violation of the Paris Agreements; harder to counter with B-52s, which Thieu apparently expected would be forthcoming in case of an overt and unmistakable major violation; and therefore harder to foil.

Contrast with French-Vietnamese Relations

Some respondents emphasized that the differences between the Vietnamese and the Americans were not like the differences between them and the French, which were in fact profound conflicts over aims and objectives. Some respondents attribute the failures of fruitful cooperation with the United States primarily to American misperceptions of *everything* they found in Vietnam: the country, the people, the culture, the war, the enemy. While veterans of the American military or civilian bureaucracy often place the blame for this lack of understanding on the absence of "institutional memory," which resulted from personnel rotation, most Vietnamese held quite a different view. They saw the chasm as deeper than that. Curiously enough, some respondents felt that on the level of the combat soldier, where ignorance regarding Vietnam was perhaps greatest, interaction was perhaps most effective. According to one general:

> Throughout the whole hierarchy, it should be noted that the best and smoothest interaction existed at the lowest echelons, at company and battalion levels, where the personalities involved were younger, more innocent and devoid of scheming of any sort. There the cooperation was frank, the spirit of camaraderie was more instinctive, and the proximity of the physical dangers experienced together on the battlefield further deepened the closeness between the U.S. and Vietnam.
>
> At the middle echelons the difficulties in interaction were greatest, the personalities involved being no longer candid and disinterested, and yet not completely mature in judgments and attitudes.
>
> And finally at the higher echelons, including the JGS, I would

certainly not envy the position of the Americans who were obligated to work with such incompetent counterparts, with naturally some rare exceptions.

Another general, who also held high civilian office at times, summed up the matter by saying, "We did not have the feeling of a common goal." He felt, further, as did other respondents, that the Americans generally underestimated the dangers in the situation, never contemplating that the war might end with a complete Communist victory. He conceded that most Vietnamese leaders never really contemplated such a possibility either, but for other reasons: They were confident that in case of need, American help would ultimately materialize to prevent such a disaster.

The Military Advisers System

The concept of military advisers was criticized by several of the respondents. One critic said that as long as the Vietnamese had American advisers on all levels, the Americans should have had, and heeded, Vietnamese advisers. Had such a system been practiced, he thought, My Lai could not have occurred and there would have been fewer incidents of the type that fueled resistance to the war in the United States and around the world. When asked for his personal opinion of one of the most famous senior U.S. advisers, one respondent said, "Well [laughter], he was overbearing. He did not understand the situation very well. He was not profound enough. He did not go to the root of the problem. And he thought he knew everything."

Marshal Ky was even more explicit on the adviser system:

> After a few years, there is some sort of Mafia established between American advisers and the Vietnamese commanding officers because, you know, they need each other to get promotions, they need good records and recommendation. What is the best record for an American adviser? Serving one, two tours with a Vietnamese unit. If, after that, he came back and can show the American Headquarters that here is a unit I advised for a year and now it is a Number One outfit, he shares that merit. Every American adviser

when they left . . . to go back to the United States have all kinds of Vietnamese decorations [laughter], and vice versa . . . I know one general officer, the commanding officer of a Corps, later on Thieu removed him, General Ngo Dzu of II Corps. He's a coward; he's involved in all kind of smuggling and corruption, but still many Americans, when they come to me, they say, you know, Dzu is a "number one" type. Unbelievable.

Ky also suggested that Americans often had the wool pulled over their eyes:

When [an] American visitor came to Corps headquarters I don't think he really saw much except to spend time drinking, eating and girls with the Corps commander and after that, you know, for the American visitor, [that Corps commander] is "number one."

Ky also accused Americans of having had an insatiable appetite for "yes men" and added that "leadership cannot be built that way."

The military was said by some respondents to have resented the direct influence the Americans exerted on the promotion of high-ranking (and sometimes lower-level) officers, not so much because of the interference itself, it seems, as because of the criteria used by Americans to support a Vietnamese officer. The Americans, these respondents said, judged a man too easily on whether he spoke decent English and drank some bourbon with them; and the Americans could be fooled into declaring some man a "tiger" when in fact he was nothing of the kind. Marshal Ky gave what he considered an example, with unmistakable relish: "As long as they [the Americans] praise a military leader like Dzu and call him "number one tiger," what do they know about Vietnamese officers? Most of the Americans I talked to think he's number one tiger [loud laughter], but I am eyewitness: Dzu came running to my home, a shaken chicken!"

The Americans also failed to understand, according to one respondent, that age in an officer meant something else in ARVN than it meant in the U.S. Army. In the U.S. Army it could mean maturity and experience, whereas in ARVN it could mean a rigid clinging to outmoded tactics learned in school and, even worse, a history of involvement with the French and therefore a contamination that made the officer uninspiring as a leader in the current war.

In their complaints about American interference in Vietnamese affairs, the respondents said that there had been too much interference and at the same time too little. According to them, the Americans interfered often in the wrong ways or places. Among themselves, the Vietnamese called the U.S. Ambassador "the governor" even though, to their surprise, "the governor" occasionally sought their help in tasks they were clearly unable to perform. For example, the Ambassador would ask them to help in inducing Thieu to do something that he himself could not induce Thieu to do. This reflected a grossly unrealistic appraisal of the situation on the part of the Ambassador, in the view of these witnesses.

Bui Diem reported:

> I remember . . . in the early seventies, each time I had . . . opportunities to talk to Ambassador Bunker, he urged me to take up the problem of the reforms with the Vietnamese President. "You should mention to the President that reforms are badly needed both for the strengthening of your defense posture and for improving the atmosphere in Washington, a condition for the U.S. to continue its support." Trying to convince Mr. Thieu about the necessity to reorganize his government I had done all along, but in terms of influence on him, there definitely was no comparison between my position as Ambassador and the position of the U.S. Ambassador in Saigon. If, with the tremendous bargaining power he had in his hands, the U.S. Ambassador could not do anything to influence Mr. Thieu, how could I?

Yet, when the Americans left, their departure also caused the Vietnamese some distress: Many of the jobs that had been provided by the American presence, particularly in Saigon, disappeared. This added to the economic plight experienced by many in that city. Second, the men on the higher levels, especially in the military, found that they had come to rely on the American decision-making and decision-implementing machinery which now had disappeared. The Commander of I Corps, Lieutenant General Ngo Quang Truong, for example, noted that after the U.S. withdrawal, command and control from Saigon became weak, as did planning. He added that this shortcoming should have been remedied while the U.S. forces were still in Vietnam.

An example of the criticism that the Americans interfered in the wrong ways is given in the following excerpt from an interview with a high-ranking staff officer:

Q. What mistakes do you think the Americans made in preparing South Vietnam to fight this war?

A. Two things. First, when American troops came to Vietnam, they try to do everything. And make the Vietnamese lose the initiative.

Q. This happened on all levels?

A. Yes, I think at all levels—operations, training, logistics. So the Vietnamese don't rely on themselves. They rely on the Americans.

Q. The Americans were doing the planning?

A. Yes, but short planning, just for one year only. You didn't know how much you can get next year of American financial aid.

Q. We ran things. Is that the problem?

A. Yes. Sometimes the Americans try to get suggestions from the Vietnamese side, but we have no competent people to deal with the American side. So the Americans think: We will do it for you because you don't know anything. And second, U.S. supports one man only— President Thieu.

Q. What should we have done?

A. Well, I think instead of total support you have to tell him if you don't open your arms, your hand, to [accept] contribution from good people, I can't support you.

Colonel Do Ngoc Nhan, who served on the JGS in the final days, stated that "the U.S. got involved in the war and assumed the leadership both politically and militarily. For this reason, the U.S. withdrawal from South Vietnam created a real leadership vacuum." Yet the Americans apparently faced a Hobson's choice in Vietnam: When they asserted their leadership, it allegedly restricted the development of Vietnamese leadership and had other adverse effects; but when they did not exert their leadership, this was felt to have had adverse consequences, too. Besides, leadership responsibilities devolved on the Americans simply because their presence was so heavy. Bui Diem commented:

> More than anything else, the South Vietnamese blamed the Americans for the many contradictions of the American policy. . . . The South Vietnamese could not understand why the Americans tried to assert that there was no interference on their part in South Vietnamese politics, as if they could avoid it in practice after imposing the presence of five hundred thousand American troops on the country.

Such a presence, said Diem, had "its pros and cons and many Vietnamese were aware of it." The point was that on the one hand the American presence was a substantial help, but on the other, it diluted the "cause." Diem said:

> The Communists . . . boasted about the purity and legitimacy of their cause (fight for total independence of the country and against the presence of foreign troops), and the South Vietnamese did not want to carry this handicap (of relying on foreign troops) on their back. However, they accepted the presence of American troops as justified by the international circumstances and the rapidly deteriorating situation in South Vietnam. There was, after all, a ferocious war going on and there was no substitute for victory even if the cost was to be some sort of foreign interference.

In other words, American support, even when it was militarily effective, was not an unmixed blessing, according to this observer. The enemy, of course, even though he was maneuvering between

87

Moscow and Peking and therefore may have seemed to possess a modicum of independence, was solidly dependent on foreign support, too. However, he had the advantage of having no foreign troops in his ranks, and his allies, according to the respondents, disguised their influence quite effectively, whereas the United States did not. One respondent complained:

> When South Vietnam scored a success, Americans took the credit. When the North scored a success it was always Ho Chi Minh or Giap or the NVA that got the credit.

Disagreements on Force Structure

The severest criticism on the part of several Vietnamese military men with regard to U.S.-Vietnamese cooperation was that the American forces left the military forces of South Vietnam unprepared to fight the war by themselves, that the Americans in fact did, in many respects, the reverse of what would have been required. The respondents' views on this subject are reflected in the following summary of their comments:

1. The South Vietnamese soldier was "conditioned" by the U.S. presence in many wrong ways. He had become accustomed to vast air and artillery support, and he had "forgotten how to walk," having become used to motorized transportation.
2. ARVN was organized along the wrong pattern. Some of the "young Turks" among the respondents said that ARVN should have consisted of two distinctly separate parts with distinctly separate missions: It should have had a territorial force, entrusted with the defense of their territory, and a large and mobile strike force that could have been used wherever needed. Instead, it did not have any mobile reserve divisions, and it had far too big a "tail."
3. The armed forces of South Vietnam were not enabled to develop effective military leaders at the top. A great many

direct and indirect reasons were given for this. The promotion process was determined to a large extent by corruption and the "crony" system. Prima donnas without formal training were entrusted with the most responsible positions, such as Corps commands, where they "improvised like artists without having learned the fundamentals." Commanders given U.S. schooling got very little benefit from it; there was too much, too fast. Moreover, what little they did learn did not apply to the situation in Vietnam, where the enemy and the terrain required a different type of warfare than that taught at American defense colleges.

The worst feature of ARVN, according to one JGS colonel, was that it was not an independent entity and could not quickly become one after the American departure. The colonel advocated a mobile force of 10 to 15 divisions:

> I don't know if you agree with me, but this is my opinion. The Vietnamese armed forces were totally integrated in the whole U.S. military machine and were just part of that structure. So, when the whole U.S. armed forces got out, the Vietnamese forces could not really sustain themselves against a hard blow. . . . We were integrated in the whole U.S. armed forces. When the [bigger] part of that integrated force leaves, the remaining Vietnam forces have lack of support, lack of leadership, lack of coordination. Their mission is . . . to hold ground and they can counter some small action by the other side but [that is all]. We cannot put together one division to do something. And if we can get one division together we cannot do anything because they don't have the support to do it. So the capability of the Vietnamese forces [after the U.S. withdrawal] was just to hold ground and counter very small enemy activity.

Did the colonel talk to the Americans about this?

> Not officially. But during the time when I was Chief of Staff of the Training Command, I had the opportunity to talk with a lot of American generals, a lot of American diplomats. I told them we

cannot operate this way. The structure of ARVN is not operational when the Americans go. We have to do something. What I propose is this [the 10 to 15 mobile divisions]. But it will take time to do it. We have to do this right, and should have started in 1966/67 to do this right.

When asked what kind of response he received, the colonel stated:

The Vietnamese said they did not want to hear anything about this because now the Americans were responsible for everything. But it was also very difficult to talk to the Americans. Because, as you know, the Americans have their own system and we are talking about something that is [outside] that system.

As an afterthought, he added:

Also, [the Americans were not sympathetic to his view] because they thought they can stay in Vietnam forever.

But, according to the colonel, nobody worried very much about faulty ARVN policies because it was generally expected that in case of need the Americans would come to the rescue. Without the Americans, he thought, there was no chance, anyway. Like others, he stated that even Thieu believed that:

Q. Thieu believed the Americans would bail out Vietnam in case of problems?

A. Yes. I think Thieu knew that once you made a withdrawal it was finished, with . . . [what] the enemy had.

Q. You think Thieu believed it was finished when the Americans withdrew?

A. Yes. Because Thieu really is a shrewd man, he is intelligent and he is a military leader, he would know this.

Thus, here again, we see the ambivalent attitude toward the Americans that, according to the respondents, was so widespread among Vietnamese leaders: On the one hand, the Americans were hard to deal with and pressed for the wrong ways to build up ARVN; on the other, they could surely be counted on if things went wrong.

A "People's Army"?

During the war there was talk from time to time about the concept of a "people's army" for South Vietnam, in American and Vietnamese quarters. Lieutenant General Tran Van Don was one of the leading proponents of this concept. The people's army was an idea advanced by those who doubted that South Vietnam could support the costly military machine and lavish fighting style that South Vietnam was bequeathed by the Americans. Drawn from Vietnam's own military history, the people's army would have been built upon the principle of local self-defense. Every able-bodied man and woman would serve a fixed tour of duty with the armed forces, after which they would return to civilian production jobs, remaining in an armed reserve to defend their own locality or to augment the regular forces when needed. The regular army would thus be free for larger operations against the North Vietnamese. With part-time soldiers and part-time producers, the people's army, it was felt, would ease the economic and manpower burden of maintaining South Vietnam's large armed forces while still maintaining the country's defense needs. A people's army was something between the Minutemen of the American Revolution and the Israeli reserve system, but the idea predated both. It was with such an organization that Vietnam had historically defended its frontiers and developed its territory.

An idea similar to that of a people's army had apparently been expressed by the commander of the 1st Infantry Division. According to one of his subordinates in the 1st Division, this general had spoken about reducing the strength of the army's support units and putting some of their men into the Regional Forces and Popular Forces, which would be reorganized as "Rice Producer Units." "When the situation is favorable and quiet," he reportedly said, "they can work in the ricefields, and when there is increased enemy activity, they fight."

The people's army concept was not accepted by many, however. Buu Vien dismissed the idea:

> In the aftermath of the Vietnam debacle, some people have severely criticized the government of the RVN for not having organized "a people-based army"; of not knowing how to fight a war with less costly expenditures; of having relied too much on foreign assistance, etc. . . . There might have been some justification in this so far as people's motivation is concerned, but the outcome would have been the same.

A South Vietnamese army officer also thought the idea inapplicable to South Vietnam. "It sounds good but it is not logical from the standpoint of strategic analysis. . . . To use the 'Rice Producer Units' in case we need them will not be easy. Israel can do it that way, but South Vietnam can't. In Israel, they have a very low percentage of enemy infrastructure in the population. I'd say none. But in South Vietnam this element is very great. . . . If the Communists will find out that is our concept, they will not attack us, but just harass the 'Rice Producer Units' every night and day. How can they produce?"

Overview

To this brief summary of Vietnamese views on U.S.-Vietnamese relations we should add the statements of one high-ranking combat officer who insisted on remaining anonymous. This respondent insisted that South Vietnam, which in his view was viable politically and militarily and could have successfully "fought the enemy a hundred years" if it had been "permitted" to do so, had been traded away to Hanoi by the Americans in return for better relations with Moscow and Peking. He stated that the United States had actually pulled the strings to insure the quick defeat of South Vietnam. Pursuing the point, the interviewer asked him, "In other words, you mean to say that in order to have better relations with China and maybe the Soviet Union the people in the United States wanted to sell out Vietnam? Is that what you mean?"

The officer answered, "I don't mean all the people in the United States." The interviewer then asked, "You mean some of the people in the United States? Who? In the government?" "Sure, policymakers—people like that," said the respondent. Asked again, "But do you really believe that a trade was made at some point where Mr. Kissinger would go to Mr. Brezhnev or Mr. Mao and say, 'If you give me such and such, I will give you South Vietnam'?" The general replied, "My answer is yes!" This respondent also insisted that he was not alone among exiled leaders in holding this view but that the others "are afraid to tell you."

The other factor that was mentioned by some respondents, though often only peripherally or by insinuation, was that the all-pervading and all-corroding corruption was to some extent, at least indirectly, the fault of the Americans: As long as the United States supported President Thieu in his position of leadership, and with him "Fat Quang" and all the others, there was no way of reducing the corruption. Marshal Ky was most outspoken on this and reported that he made the point so strongly in a conversation with President Nixon that Ambassador Bui Diem "kicked him under the table." But nothing came of this.[10]

Despite the great hostility displayed by the respondent who claims South Vietnam was betrayed, despite Nguyen Ba Can's statement that "Vietnamese officials called Vietnamization the U.S. Dollar and Vietnam Blood Sharing Plan," and despite much criticism of American ways and means, the Vietnamese leaders did not, on the whole, respond as "angry men" to the question of U.S.-Vietnamese relations. Rather, they seemed to feel that fate was against a more fruitful cooperation between their nation and the Americans. They did not appear to give credence to the Communist claim that the Americans in Vietnam were motivated by the same imperialist desires as the French had been before them. On the contrary, some seemed to feel that the Americans really wanted to help but did so very poorly, whereas the French

[10] The authors are aware that Ky himself has often been accused of corruption, but he was not challenged on this during the interview. Respondents were repeatedly challenged on facts. However, they were not challenged on such points as personal conduct.

(with whom, however, they now are reconciled and to whom they feel culturally closer) meant to exploit them and did quite well at that, for a long time. The respondents simply stressed, in their polite and seemingly dispassionate way, that U.S.-Vietnamese interaction was caught in many webs of misunderstanding from the beginning and never improved, eventually dissolving altogether.

Chapter 5

Strategy and Tactics

Strategy and Tactics

After the Americans left, Thieu promulgated his "Four No's," one of which was to deny the enemy any territory or outpost held by the GVN (as stated earlier, the other three no's were no coalition government, no negotiating with the enemy, and no Communist or neutralist activity in the country). The territorial no was the conceptual and operational backbone of South Vietnam's military posture from the time of the Paris Agreements until after the fall of Ban Me Thuot, when it was radically revised and, in fact, entirely reversed.

As it turned out, the "no surrender of any territory" strategy was a miscalculation in all respects, according to the interviews. Even though the cease-fire violations by the enemy did stand out by contrast, as the South Vietnamese leaders hoped they would, the United States did not do anything to punish the enemy, which, the respondents say, greatly discouraged them and encouraged the enemy to risk ever bigger violations.[11] Thus the relative observance of the cease-fire by the GVN went unrewarded. Holding on to all territory might have served in some measure to reassure the population, except that—as we learned from Nguyen Ba Can and many others—the population largely turned against the Thieu government in the final crisis anyway and denied it the needed support. And as for propitiating the Americans and extracting more aid from them by showing Saigon's ability to deny the enemy new territory after the Paris Agreements, the record shows that the

[11] See footnote 2.

GVN's relative success on that score did not keep U.S. aid to South Vietnam from declining drastically.

Thus, none of the political objectives at which the Thieu strategy had aimed was accomplished in the period between the Paris Agreements and the final enemy offensive. Instead, according to some of the respondents, the rigid strategic posture had weakened the military establishment and produced other adverse military consequences. It had led to a firm commitment of all available forces to the defense of their respective areas, so that these forces had no strategic mobility and ARVN had no strategic reserves. Besides, according to the officers interviewed for this study, these forces lacked transport and fuel, so they were virtually nailed to their places, and any effort at redeploying them, like Thieu's last-minute attempt to move the Airborne Division down to Saigon from I Corps, disrupted the entire defense posture from I Corps on down. Moreover, the attempt to hold on to every one of thousands of remote outposts apparently ground up both the armed forces *and* the morale of officers who saw the virtual hopelessness of such an endeavor but were committed to it.

What seems to emerge quite clearly from the combined statements of the respondents is that the strategy of passive defense,[12] coupled with a decline in U.S. military aid, led to increasing human losses. With ARVN's increasing need to conserve ammunition and POL, and with maintenance problems and other technological adversities, the brunt of the enemy's forays had to be borne increasingly by the ARVN soldier. This required increasing sacrifices in men as the enemy's capabilities kept improving along with the quality of his equipment.

However, the rigidity of Thieu's strategy was not just the result of his own ideas and desires, nor was it dictated by the situation, at least not according to all respondents. Some respondents believed that it was "imposed" on Thieu by the Americans. The last South Vietnamese Minister of Defense, Tran Van Don, commented in his interview:

[12] Actually, the tactics were not entirely passive, as both sides "fought viciously" over some territories, according to one officer.

Q. What were the plans? How was South Vietnam going to survive militarily?

A. You ask me, personally?

Q. From the point of view of the government, the JGS, or whoever might have discussed this with you, did they have a plan or a strategy?

A. I know, as Chairman of the Defense Committee in the House before becoming a Vice-Premier in 1974 . . . the military strategy at that time was to hold all of South Vietnam. I asked Thieu in 1975 why in Cam Ranh "you have changed your strategy?" He said, "Now with open aggression from the North we cannot keep the same strategy demanded by the American side to hold the whole of South Vietnam."

Q. He said that was the American strategy? Americans had asked him to do this?

A. To keep, to hold all the whole South Vietnam. He was able to change [that] after the attack from the North.

Q. He said that was an American strategy, imposed on him by the U.S.?

A. Yes. Important to hold all South Vietnam and, if possible, all provinces.

But even though Tran Van Don stated that the strategy of holding on to all areas was dictated by the Americans, he by no means attributed to them all responsibility for what came later, nor did he feel that the South Vietnamese did not have enough freedom of action to do things differently.

A. I knew the preparations made by the other side—pipeline, new highway, attacks against our districts, infiltration into the South—even then we didn't prepare our troops, our army, to fight. We had no big operation to destroy the pipeline, to go in where . . . they occupied.

99

Q. No spoiling action?

A. That's right.

Q. Would you attribute that to inept leadership?

A. Yes, of course. We come back again to the same thing. I was surprised. We look [as though] we live in peacetime. Instead, we know about the infiltration, the attacks . . . I don't mean after the loss of Phuoc Long Province, but before that—in 1974—the pipeline, the highway, infiltration. We knew that. Lack of command, incompetence on our military side. From the top to the division commander and province chief.

Q. You think you had the resources . . . to mount some spoiling operations?

A. We come back again to the same problem [of] Thieu. If they open real operations, it will require good commanders, good operations, it could have happened. But for Thieu, the danger was there would be a coup against him.

While Don indicated that Thieu did not want good men in leading military positions because he was afraid that once they were in such positions they would mount a coup against him, there was more than that to the absence of more vigorous defense strategies:

Q. Your judgment is that there was a sort of peacetime attitude while this [enemy] buildup was taking place?

A. Yes, that is right. There is one thing I think these leaders believed—the American government will never permit a new aggression from the North after the Paris Agreements. Bombing will be resumed.

But long before 1975, Don had been troubled by the strategies and tactics used in the war, not only by his own compatriots but by the Americans as well:

When I used to drive through the pass from Danang to Hue, I could see American GIs playing the role of our Popular Forces, guarding all the bridges. . . . Some bridges are important. [But] why didn't I see any Vietnamese with them? There was something wrong in the use of American troops during the war. I thought they were not very well employed.

In general, no strategy could have been successful, in General Don's view, unless it effectively stopped the infiltration from the North. Don thought that could have been done, but only through a major mobilization of all forces available in the country. The attempts that were made he dismissed as "not serious." He commented on the operation at Lam Son in 1971 that was designed to cut infiltration:

Not very well conducted on the Vietnamese side. General Lam was the Corps Commander. He had his command post in Dong Ha, but every evening he flew back to Danang to play tennis. Every morning he came back to his CP. . . . No coordination with the General Staff, no coordination with General Abrams. General Abrams was so nice . . . he didn't want to complain.

Others also deplored the absence of efforts to stop the infiltration. General Ngo Quang Truong said in hindsight that halting infiltration was the most critical requirement. He said that South Vietnam could have solved its internal problems if the infiltration could have been brought under control. Once that had been stopped, everything else would have been "easy." When asked how the infiltration might have been stopped, he said that the geography was not the same as that in Korea and it would have required "strong retaliation" to keep the enemy at bay. This, presumably, would have meant coercive bombing of the North.

But, if there were no serious efforts at stopping the infiltration, what *was* the overall strategy? Tran Van Don had this to report:

You know, General Vien, the chairman of the JGS, talked to me once in the beginning of 1969 when I was Chairman of the Defense Committee of the Senate and I led a delegation of Senators and members of the House to the General Staff headquarters, to Cao

101

Van Vien's office. Our question was, "General, can you tell us (we are now members of the House and Senate in a very close meeting) your military doctrine because we need to know. We are making war, but on the basis of what doctrine?" That question was very good. It was very sensible. It was not my question, it was the question of the other members. We agreed on that question. Do you know what the answer was from Cao Van Vien? He said, "We Vietnamese have no military doctrine because the command of all operations in Vietnam is in the hands, is the responsibility, of the American side. We follow the U.S. military doctrine. We cannot have a Vietnamese military doctrine. We can get it only on the day when we will be in charge, when we will be responsible for the operations in South Vietnam." That is all. That means we follow. I have just told you about the Lam Son operation just to show you, to describe to you, the lack of coordination; I don't say "cooperation," but coordination between the U.S. and Vietnamese sides. And I must say to you that sometimes some of your generals were very happy to have a nice Vietnamese counterpart who never reacted against any decision made by the American side. It was easier for the American general not to review what he had decided already or else had planned by his staff. Sometimes he said, "Oh, this Vietnamese general is very fine." Of course, of course, he would say that. You know, if we are to be frank, we must be frank.

However, from what the respondents said, "on the day they were in charge," the Vietnamese JGS did not evolve a strategy either.

The respondents largely agreed that the JGS was very weak, in concepts and in personnel, and did not become any stronger when the Americans left. Its chief, often described by the respondents as very "passive," remained in place; the Corps commanders, directly responsible to Thieu, retained control over their fiefdoms while they tried to defend them against the enemy; Thieu bypassed the JGS; and no planning staff worth the name generated any doctrines or strategies for the conduct of the war. According to some respondents, the Chairman of the JGS, General Vien, had tendered his resignation to Thieu on several occasions, as he did not want the job. But Thieu, it is said, was very happy with Vien, who was accommodating and certainly never entertained any ideas

102

of mounting or participating in a coup. One JGS officer who kept pressing for alternate force postures said:

> General Vien did nothing, and it was very hard to reach him. And any time people asked him something, he said, "Go to the Corps commanders and get direct instructions from President Thieu. Our mission is not to mount big operations, so the Province chief and the Corps commander have responsibility for the security of their area. That is all." And General Vien did nothing . . . even to the last day in Saigon. . . . That was because he didn't want the job. He wanted to quit for a long time and no one would let him go. He submitted his resignation seven times and they would not let him go. The reasons? I think that General Vien was good for Thieu. I think that in Thieu's mind the Americans were responsible for everything and the Vietnamese did not need to do anything. And everyone just sit down and wait because they think the Americans have the responsibility for everything.

The unfavorable reaction of the respondent in this case was produced by Vien's negative response to his suggestion that ARVN forces be repostured so as to get out of their static defense positions and aim at a more active strategy.

Why Was There No Strategic Planning?

In most conversations, respondents made it clear that there was little strategic planning; that, in fact, Saigon, which had no strategy of its own when the Americans were in the country, also failed to develop a real strategy after they had left. When asked about the reasons for this, considering the obviously precarious situation in which the South found itself, and considering the ubiquitous conviction in all South Vietnamese circles that the enemy would never regard the Paris Agreements as anything but the proverbial scrap of paper, these respondents pointed to their weak and ineffective General Staff, their poor and unimaginative leadership, or the unfortunate conditioning of their leaders by the Americans.

Some reported that they had plans for different force structures and strategies but could never get a hearing, let alone authorization to act. But again and again, respondents insisted that there was no real strategy because, first, they were persuaded that the United States would come to their aid in case of real need, and, second, there simply was no strategy they could possibly design that would enable them to go it alone if a big enemy push should materialize:

Q. You say, each year you had a plan, first, you had a joint plan with MACV. After the Americans left you had a Vietnamese plan. And that plan said that each Corps commander was responsible . . .

A. To protect his area, protect the people and what they are to do about pacification, about the roads, etc. But this plan never mentions what to do if a full attack happens.

Q. So all the plan dealt with was how the people were to be protected, pacification, roads, this kind of thing. The plan did not contemplate or deal with what he should do in the event there was a large-scale attack. Did the Corps commanders have any plans of their own, as to what they were to do?

A. Based on this overall plan, each Corps commander made his own plan, but the plan was the same as the JGS plan, which means yes, we will deploy our troops like this to protect the people, but if there were really a full-scale attack, they need some support and help from the JGS, but they know that the JGS has nothing under his command. Not even one battalion. So all the force is divided into four Corps. And the Corps commanders are responsible for what they have on hand. That is the kind of structure after 1973.

Q. So the Corps commanders would say in their plan, if there is a large attack, we will get help from Saigon? Is that what they said? Even though they knew there wasn't any help?

A. Yes, they knew that. So what I mentioned is this: All the

104

ARVN are spread out through the four Corps areas and had as their mission the protection of the people. And we [believed] that after the 1973 Agreements there would be no attack at all. But if the full attack happened the Americans would jump in. So you carry out the mission you did before with the Americans.

Q. Carry out the mission you had when the Americans were there—still carry that out. If a full attack takes place, the Americans would come to the rescue?

A. Yes.

Q. So it all came back again to the Americans?

A. I think so. Operating with the American forces—they [ARVN] cannot operate alone.

Q. Cannot operate alone?

A. Yes.

This respondent (a colonel in the JGS and a participant in the Paris negotiations) thought that the Americans must have believed that after the Paris Agreements the enemy would not dare to launch a large-scale attack, and that therefore the Saigon leaders did not plan for such a contingency:

A. Because they think that the Americans have plans about this, and they still believe that after the Agreements they cannot have a full attack from the North.

Q. You think the Americans believed that?

A. In their plans for the ARVN. Because after the Peace Agreement it was impossible to have a full attack. And if the full attack happened, it was finished. And they knew this.

Q. Now you are speaking from the Vietnamese point of view or the American point of view?

A. Both. The Americans knew this.

105

Q. You mentioned, I have forgotten who it was, a senior person, who told you when you suggested the need to do something, he said don't worry about that, the Americans will still work something out at the very end. Who was it?

A. Most of the people believed this, when I talked with all the generals, the responsible people. For example, when I got back from Paris, I went to see Khiem, the Prime Minister, and Minister of Defense, and reported to him. He asked me about the situation. I told him. He said, "Yes, I already think that. In [case of a major attack], we cannot do anything. The Americans will have to decide what we have to do." This was from Khiem.

Should South Vietnam Have Fought Like the Enemy?

Throughout the war in Vietnam, some American critics of ARVN strategies expressed the view that it was necessary to adopt the enemy's ways of fighting. One corps commander who commented on this proposition dismissed it as unrealistic. He remarked that a criticism frequently leveled against ARVN—that it should have adopted more of the enemy's tactics—was unwarranted in that ARVN "faced a different situation and could not employ the enemy's mode of operation." This officer had at one time commanded the 1st Division and had in fact used some of the enemy's tactics in certain areas. He said he was "very familiar" with Communist tactics but that they could be used only to "some extent." ARVN requirements were quite different from those of the Communists, and only a limited amount of modification was possible in their operations. The main reason ARVN could not adopt the enemy's mode of fighting, according to the respondents, was that it fought defensively, in its own country, whereas the enemy fought aggressively and not on his own territory.

Should South Vietnam Have Gone North?

Attacking North Vietnam was a recurring idea among South Vietnam's leaders. Major General Nguyen Khanh (Prime Minister from February to August 1964 and briefly President) had publicly announced a "March North" campaign in July 1964, although it was largely for propaganda purposes. Several of the respondents, however, felt that South Vietnam's armed forces should have initiated some military operations against the North as the only way to limit, and perhaps ultimately end, North Vietnam's military operations in the South. Said one senior VNAF commander, "We were not able to go up North and that is the real crux." Air Marshal Ky suggested the creation of guerrilla bases in North Vietnam to tie down North Vietnamese troops:

> . . . at the Guam Conference [held in 1967] I told General Vien to brief President Johnson and [the] American delegation about a plan to have us go North. Not [a] full invasion but to establish a set zone like the Communists had, Zone D and C down south . . . the idea was at least to have a big military camp in the mountainous area where we could defend ourselves easily, to keep the Communist troops there in the North and second, serving as a rallying point to other anti-Communist [people in the North].

Ky believed that the establishment of guerrilla zones in North Vietnam would show the North Vietnamese that the South Vietnamese "have the guts to go up there, to fight in their own territory." Second, the guerrilla zones would "rally all the population in the North." Asked by the interviewer if he actually believed that the population of the North would have rallied, Ky used an anecdote to assert that there were some friendly feelings for Saigon in the North. When pressed by the interviewer, who suggested that there was a great difference between some friendly feelings and people actually joining the other side, Ky agreed but added that the idea should at least have been tested.

Some respondents felt that landings should have been made north of the DMZ that would have destroyed forces assembled there and pinned down other forces instead of permitting them to infiltrate south. This strategy also would have offered Saigon an opportunity to foster local resistance in North Vietnam against Hanoi.[13]

Most of those who thought the South Vietnamese should have made incursions into the North added that such operations would "of course" have been possible only with massive U.S. support. Marshal Ky, on the other hand, seemed to feel that ARVN could have done some extensive probing of this kind on its own. He stated that he had repeatedly advocated this and had volunteered to lead such raids but had not prevailed.

The Wrong Expectations

Not only were there wrong expectations as to what the *United States* would do in case of a massive enemy attack, there were also wrong expectations as to what the *enemy* would do, and these contributed further to the strategic vacuum in which Saigon operated. These faulty expectations, which would have made effective strategic planning most unlikely even if other factors had not also interfered were present at the highest level—in President Thieu's own mind.

Buu Vien reported that Thieu thought that "subversion would probably be the main tool the Communists would use to seize control of the country":

> In a Ministers' Council meeting, President Thieu laid down his theories as follows: He predicted two possibilities, two courses of action which might be taken by the Communists. One would be a major military offensive on the 1972 model. The enemy would try to capture as much of our territory as possible, then negotiate another in-place cease-fire. If the offensive ever occurred, it would

---

[13] This idea indicated that the South Vietnamese leaders thought they, too, could combine warfighting with revolutionary subversion, *but only in the enemy's territory*. They could not imitate the enemy and use guerrilla tactics inside their own territory because they were fighting in defense of the established order prevailing there. The enemy could use guerrilla tactics in the South, but the South Vietnamese could have used them only in the North.

involve entire divisions, and a combination of armor, artillery and ground forces. The fighting would be violent, but it wouldn't last long. The Communists would make every effort to gain as much as possible before the U.S. could have any significant reaction. Then, facing a fait accompli, the only way out would be more negotiations. Negotiations would end up in stalemate and in the meantime, the Communists would consolidate their positions in newly occupied areas, build up strength, and get prepared for the next offensive. If this ever happened, we would expect that the U.S., a co-signatory of the cease-fire agreement, wouldn't sit on their hands but would certainly intervene. The most important thing for us would be our capability to hold out firmly and destroy as much of the enemy as possible while waiting for U.S. intervention. So the armed forces should be vigilant, leadership should be strengthened to keep troop morale high and improvement of soldiers' living conditions should be attained.

The other possible course of action of the Communists was the *real main concern of the government* [emphasis added]. That was the seizure of power through subversive tactics in which the Communists excel. . . .

Thieu then continued his prognosis as follows, according to Buu Vien:

The infiltration of the Communists at the infrastructure level would lead to the loss of control of villages by local authorities, to the sabotage and failure of government programs and eventually leave the central government isolated in cities, surrounded by a hostile countryside. Gradually, the cities would be undermined as well, aided directly or indirectly by troubles and unrest caused by opposition elements to the government. The government then might no longer effectively govern and the eventual establishment of a pro-Communist government at the instigation of the Communists and their allies would no longer be a remote possibility.

While we could rely on U.S. intervention to thwart a major Communist offensive, and the U.S. would have enough reason to intervene in case of a flagrant Communist violation of the cease-fire agreement, we couldn't rely on anybody but ourselves to save the country from a political collapse, which was considered to be totally an internal affair.

Needless to say, if those were Thieu's basic assumptions regarding future enemy actions, effective strategies were not likely to be forthcoming. As a result, pessimism appears to have prevailed in high places. Asked when he thought the war was lost, one combat commander answered, "Strategically, in 1973." "And immediately?" asked the interviewer. "After Ban Me Thuot was overrun." To Buu Vien, such comments were not evidence of unwarranted defeatism but were rather simply realistic because of the massive support enjoyed by the enemy.

A general officer, Nguyen Xuan Thinh, asked:

> What good did it do to resist when the defeat was inevitable? To prolong the war by several months, or several weeks, could only cause Vietnamese blood to be shed in vain, be it Communist or Nationalist blood.

The "Conditio Sine Qua Non"

Buu Vien placed the entire discussion about possible alternative strategies into a broader context than some of his colleagues. First, he commented on the magnitude of the task:

> It all began with the realistic expectation that without adequate American support, the country could not survive the North Vietnamese Communist aggression that was fully supported by the Communist world. For the North Vietnamese Communists, there was no substitute for complete domination of the whole country. For ideological and economic reasons, they always considered South Vietnam to be an integral part of their Communist nation, and they vowed to fight if necessary for two, three or more decades to accomplish their goal. Any compromise reached by any kind of agreement would be only a pause in their long march toward ultimate conquest.

Therefore, said Buu Vien, no strategy could succeed that was not responsive to the global situation—this was the "conditio sine qua non:"

It was not a question of requesting American aid to fight against the [Vietnamese] Communists by themselves but rather of countering the flow of aid from the Soviet Union and Communist China to the North Vietnamese Communists to help them conquer South Vietnam. Thus, if North Vietnam was provided with more weapons and ammunition from their allies, South Vietnam should also be provided with more weapons and ammunition from their allies. One of two things would have had to be done: Either South Vietnam had to get sufficient aid to match the Communist aid to North Vietnam, or international arrangements had to be made to have the Soviet Union and the People's Republic of China discontinue their aid to North Vietnam, leaving North Vietnam and South Vietnam alone. No country in the Free World could do either of those two things except the United States. Thus, when the U.S. deemed it not in their interest to get involved again in Vietnam, or when the U.S. found it too heavy a burden to engage in an aid race with the Soviet Union and Communist China, South Vietnam's collapse was inevitable. Not only the Republic of Vietnam but any other country in the Free World would have had the same fate.

The Unmentionable Subject

As long as the Vietnamese leaders were convinced that there was no way for them to counter a major enemy offensive without decisive U.S. help, or even to hold on rigidly to all their territory without being ground up, there seemed to be just one other option: to surrender some territories and assume a more flexible stance—in other words, to "lighten the ship at the top," as President Thieu is said to have later called his planned surrender of parts of I Corps.

Despite Thieu's stern refusal over the years to yield even a single outpost voluntarily to the enemy, the subject was apparently discussed at times, especially in the beginning of 1975, but never too seriously. According to a colonel of the JGS, a committee was set up in January of 1975:

We had a committee right in the JGS, to make a study of [strategic withdrawals]. I was invited to participate. But the committee

111

during three months of work did nothing . . . just talking, and we came up with nothing.

Even then, the committee could not level with Thieu:

> If Thieu had heard something like this you would get into big trouble. . . . For example, we said that in Kontum-Pleiku, try to hold with light forces and move the big forces to the coast, try to have a mobile defense in that area. Give up all this jungle area . . . but no, don't talk about this, we could get into lots of trouble with Thieu. Even then [before the offensive] all the hamlets around Kontum were under Communist control, but we have to say it is under our control. So we cannot move out . . . no one dared to tell the truth.

In any event, to surrender large segments of territory before the big enemy attack actually came was apparently virtually unthinkable. This may partly account for the fact that when the big offensive did come, no preparations had been made for the evacuation of civilians or even the withdrawal of troops. It was perhaps not just inadvertence and lack of professionalism that had led to the neglect of these vital preparations, but a strong inhibition on the part of military leaders even to think in such "defeatist" terms. "Having had the opportunity to attend most of the meetings concerning South Vietnamese policy toward the Paris Agreements," said Colonel Nhan, a member of the JGS, "my impression was that the cabinet members did not have the courage to offer objective observations on the situation. An extreme anti-Communist attitude was then the 'fashion,' to prove one's loyalty to one's government. All frank and outspoken opinions would have been called pacifist or pro-Communist."

Also, a strategy of strategic withdrawals was easier discussed than executed. When the offensive began, the enemy strained from the first to cut all usable roads, not only to prevent reinforcements from being brought up, but also to prevent precisely such a strategy, i.e., of ARVN first withdrawing and then perhaps creating a redoubt consisting of Saigon and the Delta. Thus, to even attempt a big strategic withdrawal, Saigon would have had to withdraw its forces from the northern provinces and surrender all that land and all its inhabitants *before* the enemy attacked in earnest—an almost impossible and also an unacceptable course of action, particularly in view of the apparently lingering thought in the minds of most military and civilian leaders, including Thieu, that such drastic regrouping would not be necessary because either the enemy would not dare to attack or the United States would come in and help, either with military intervention or diplomatic pressure, or both. This again closed the vicious circle of thinking about the subject.[14]

The Lack of Options

Thus, Saigon's strategic planners, to the extent that there were any and that they were active, seem really to have been in a box. According to what they say, they did not have the mobility or firepower or strategic reserves for an effective defense against strong attacks, let alone for large spoiling operations against the enemy's massive inroads. They could not surrender territory, as that meant surrendering populations to the enemy, disturbing the rest of the population, acting against perceived American wishes, and perhaps provoking further reductions in aid. But they also could not hold on to all the territories, because the enemy had the initiative and could strike at will, whereas South Vietnamese manpower and supplies were limited and decreasing. And they could not go north.

The only thing they could possibly do was to extract from the enemy in every engagement as high a price as possible, and some respondents feel that ARVN should have bent every effort to do precisely that, partly for their own honor and the maintenance of their own morale, and partly in order to put up a good show, slow up the enemy, and perhaps reap some harvest in the form of additional U.S. aid as a reward. Actually—though this can hardly be called a strategy—they did just that in many places over the

[14] Then too, there was always the thought that a big strategic withdrawal would be regarded as a poor showing in the United States, which would lead to even less support.

years, at great sacrifice. But there was a limit to this, and it apparently was reached when the big offensive came and the soldiers' concern over the lives of their families was added to their concern over their own.

By contrast—and the contrast could hardly have been more stark—the overall strategy of the North Vietnamese was a model of simplicity and clarity, especially after the failed 1968 and 1972 offensives freed them of the delusion that they could combine a big push with a "popular uprising" in the South. Thereafter, they relied solely on purely military means, and on the clear goal of termination through victory by conquest.

Chapter 6

Manpower and Morale

Manpower and Morale

Even though problems of manpower and problems of morale are different in many ways, they are related and were, it seems, particularly so in the Vietnam war. Due to the limitations on what superior firepower and technology could achieve during much of the war, the demands on the manpower of the contestants and the individual soldiers—both enemy and friendly—were disproportionately high.

Manpower

Perhaps the most knowledgeable of the respondents in the area of military manpower was Buu Vien, the Assistant Minister of Defense for manpower from 1972 until 1973. Somewhat tartly, Buu Vien stated:

> Because of the cease-fire agreement, foreign supporters [the United States] believed there was no reason why the Republic of Vietnam still had to maintain the 1.1 million men strength authorized in wartime. Even though they might realize that the Communist threat was still there and South Vietnam might have reason to maintain its military strength, they were more interested in restoring economic stability than in the possibility of a renewed attack by the North Vietnamese Communists. Goals were set [in 1973] at bringing down ARVN strength to 800,000 by 1976, reducing it by 100,000 each year beginning in 1974. One of the problems encountered was how troop reduction would affect the

117

respective strength of the three branches of the armed forces. . . .
Doing away with all the Popular Forces would still not be enough,
and thus a reduction in the Regional Forces and Regular Forces was
also contemplated.

This created many problems. Buu Vien reported:

> On the occasion of President Thieu's visit to the U.S. in 1973, I had
> the opportunity to brief Secretary Richardson about the plan . . .
> but when [Richardson] queried Thieu as to when the plan would go
> into effect, President Thieu replied that it all depended on the
> Communist side. . . .

Further discussions with Pentagon officials produced no solution as to how the projected reduction should be apportioned
among the services. Back in Saigon, Buu Vien—in one of those
instances where the Vietnamese appeared to have received different signals from different Americans—was told by the Defense
Attaché's Office:

> Since requests for Military Assistance for the 1974 fiscal year had
> been calculated and submitted on the basis of the 1.1 million
> strength level, it would be appropriate to maintain that level of
> strength for the time being; any reduction in strength would be
> followed by a reduction in material and equipment. As a result, the
> plan was not put into effect.

But, in what appears to have been a bit of fiscal legerdemain,
"the idea [of strength reduction] was nevertheless sold by the
government to try to attract foreign economic assistance." More
importantly, Buu Vien said:

> Even though the Saigon government well understood that the war
> against the Communists might . . . last for decades, no long-range
> policy was adopted . . . as far as use of manpower was concerned.
> . . . The general Mobilization Law enacted . . . in 1968 was
> merely a device to . . . draft younger males to serve. . . . The
> number of 18-year-olds drafted under the law . . . rarely exceeded

the 100,000 per year mark while the desertion rate usually ran much higher than that. The law was presented as a progressive piece of legislation aiming at providing everybody with an opportunity to serve the country. In reality, it was a discriminatory law whose enforcement . . . due to several clauses on draft deferments, created two categories of citizens: those who were forced into the army and those fortunate enough to stay out.

The most important shortcoming of the draft law was that it had no provision for a limited term of service [tour of duty]. Lawmakers wanted to emphasize the pressing needs of the country, and a set term of service would, they thought, appear incompatible with the "general mobilization" spirit. The only discharge from the military permitted under the law was retirement because of age. Thus, once drafted a youngster had to stay in the army until he was killed or became too old to fight. The only alternative was desertion. Draft dodging was therefore widespread, and it is obvious what happened to the morale of the draftees who saw no hope for returning to civilian life. Many youngsters even resorted to self-mutilation to escape military service.

The other flaw in the law was its provision for too many cases of draft deferment. Besides the normal deferment on grounds of poor health, deferment could also be obtained for religious reasons, for education purposes, or because of essential jobs in the public or private sector. The deferment system helped develop new corruption practices and the trade in draft deferment certificates flourished. Many youngsters shaved their heads to become fake monks, and students paid large sums of money to buy their high school diplomas or be admitted to universities.

Buu Vien reported that he discussed these matters on several occasions on the highest levels, but Thieu would not agree to a limited tour of duty or other manpower reforms.

Corruption, draft dodging, and desertion were a result of the manpower policy and in turn led to further problems of inducting young men into the army. Even when men were inducted, the army could not be certain that they were actually in the ranks; "ghost soldiers" on the one hand and "roll-call soldiers" on the other kept manpower at low and uncertain levels. Late in the war, an investigation into these practices was conducted:

119

Q. In IV Corps, you are talking about 30,000 ghost soldiers out of how many total?

A. I don't remember the figure exactly, out of about 150,000 Regional Forces.

Q. Were the other 120,000 in fact there?

A. No. Even out of the 120,000 remaining, not at all. But we didn't have time to investigate everything.

Q. When did you conduct this investigation?

A. This was about the end of 1974 and beginning of 1975.

Q. You said that these 30,000 ghost soldiers were worth 7 to 9 million piasters a month, down in IV Corps. Do you think the IV Corps Commander was getting part of this?

A. Yes.

Q. And everybody is getting paid off up and down the line?

A. Yes. And everybody knew about this in 1973-1974.

After the investigation, this respondent proposed to General Dong Van Khuyen, the Chief of Staff, that he "deactivate all these low strength battalions and fire all those battalion commanders and just form strong companies." But "instead they put them together to become regiments. So they further weakened the units."[15]

According to the respondent, a colonel in the JGS, the problem of the ghost soldiers was unsolvable for the following reasons:

Q. Why was this [ghost soldier problem]?

A. Very simple. First, the province chief will not talk back to the national leadership. Thieu only wants his own man to be province chief. . . . The province chief, he has the political responsibility, the military responsibility, everything. . . . And they divide the money among

---

[15] Lieutenant General Thinh, Commanding General of the Artillery Command, complained that the same counterproductive move toward consolidation was made with the artillery units, against his recommendations.

everyone. But we could not replace the province chief, that would come up to Thieu.

Q. You could not do anything about this?

A. You couldn't do anything about this. Just forget it.

Q. Thieu protected them?

A. Yes. And all the big bosses were protected and if you touch them you would be fired.

Thus, the manpower policies were not well suited to bring about maximum mobilization; the high desertion rate (over 100,000 a year) often more than negated the number of new draftees; and the problem of ghost soldiers and payroll soldiers further diminished effective strength and created uncertainty as to how many effectives there really were.

Morale

According to most respondents, the morale of the ARVN soldier was adversely affected by so many factors that it is remarkable that he was able to fight at all. This holds particularly true for the period when most of the American forces had left and U.S. military aid was declining in volume. Combat conditions had become much worse because not only had the umbrella of U.S. airpower and artillery support disappeared, but ARVN's own artillery and mortar units had become very severely restricted with regard to the expenditure of ammunition. This, according to the Vietnamese, led to an increase in combat losses. And, as mentioned earlier, the decline in POL and spares decreased the Med-Evac capabilities to the point where, as one deputy Corps commander put it, "many soldiers died unnecessarily."

Then, as Buu Vien pointed out above, due to the mobilization system, "a youngster, once drafted, had to stay in the army until he was killed or became too old to fight." Besides, according to Buu Vien, the draft laws were discriminatory. And the war itself certainly gave no promise of early termination.

But there was more. A high-ranking Marine officer said with bitterness:

> Yeah, you are a soldier, you are a squad leader with your squad, and you get the order to defend a hill to the death. You cannot defend to the death, when every week you hear from your family that they don't have enough food to eat. And you look back to Saigon, the rich had food, liquor, they have money, they relax, have a good time. Why fight to the death? For whom?

According to General Thinh, the morale of the soldiers was put to a severe test by yet another factor:

> The principal weakness of the South Vietnamese artillery was the extreme vulnerability of its fire bases. A single enemy mortar shell was enough to set an entire ammunition dump on fire and if the dump exploded the entire position was out of action. . . . And frequently the fall of the artillery positions led to the defeat of the units which they supported.

The Remote Commanders

One of the most important factors in maintaining the morale of soldiers—the proximity and direct leadership of competent and courageous commanders—was often absent, according to one senior general:

> Having at their disposition the most modern means of communication and transportation, signal equipment and helicopters, the field commanders, while being able to control a larger operational zone, did not have to stay constantly with their troops. They therefore failed to identify with their units, and the "esprit de corps" suffered greatly. The commanders lost the feeling for the battlefield and for their own troops, mentally and physically.

This had adverse consequences on the conduct of the war in general: "This phenomenon [of leaders being so distant] clearly explains the failure of these field commanders to react soundly when facing critical situations, and their reluctance to share dangers and hardships with their troops during the Communist offensives in 1972 and 1975." And the practice apparently depressed morale, as well:

> It was common usage that in case of heavy fighting the commanders took off in their helicopters, leaving the fighting to the troops on the ground. This had a very negative effect on troop morale. In such situations, the physical presence of the commander is greatly needed, yet the troops rarely saw their commander, they only saw his helicopter high above them, or heard only his voice through the highly sophisticated communications system. Thus the image of the commander became something very remote and very unreal to troops. The performance of units greatly suffered from this. . . . Especially in an Oriental society where the prestige, the bravery and the wisdom of the leader are of the highest importance, these negative characteristics of leadership were very detrimental.

Finally, there are questions as to the proficiency of the soldiers in combat, based on the training they had received. From what respondents reported, the various military schools were uneven in quality and were disadvantaged by interservice rivalries. These rivalries are said to have resulted in soldiers being rarely trained for interservice operations, although most actual operations were precisely of such a nature. This made the soldiers feel they had not been well trained. And yet another factor seems to have played a negative role: Some generals reported that leadership of service schools in South Vietnam was a sort of elegant exile for unwanted commanders, often of limited competence.

Thus, the ARVN soldier, from what some of the witnesses said, did not generally have the confidence of having been well trained or well led. Field commanders sometimes tended to disagree with this assessment and stated that the ARVN soldier was in fact reasonably well trained and well led, and that morale was adequate.

"Psywar"

"Indoctrination," which apparently played such a big part in the strong performance of the enemy soldiers, was another problem. There was a small "psywar" school which was expanded in 1967 into the Political Warfare College:

> But until the end of the war this college was still trying to find a logical doctrine. . . . In the Republic of China where the single party system prevails . . . the single party system would expand its control within the armed forces organizations through the Political Warfare Officers. . . . But Vietnam was different. . . . While the regime in Vietnam was hardly ideally democratic, it was far from being totalitarian. And the Political Warfare Command's organization was not affiliated with any political party. . . . Therefore the "raison d'être" of the whole organization could not really be seen.

Statements by Bui Diem and others indicated that there was a certain amount of confusion in South Vietnam as to what psywar really meant—whether it meant psychological operations against the enemy or indoctrination of friendly troops for the purpose of raising morale.[16] Some commanders apparently took it upon themselves to introduce special efforts to answer at least some of the troops' questions. Colonel Truong Tan Thuc, Deputy Commander of the elite 1st Infantry Division in I Corps, reported on such activities, also shedding some interesting light on the concerns of the combat soldiers:

> I conducted a class called Personal Problems and Questions and Answers. I was enthusiastic but also apprehensive because some of the soldiers' questions related to the "Corruption Chain" from the central government to the units in the field. The soldiers knew for sure that I knew more than they did.

Thuc then related that at the time he was conducting these classes, a local newspaper had accused the Commanding General of the 1st Division of serious corruption. When Thuc held the next session, the soldiers asked:

[16] Both operations were under the same command.

1. We, as soldiers in the field, know that you are not involved. But what do you think of this affair?
2. If the general was not involved . . . why did he not sue the newspaper for insult to his person?
3. We, soldiers in the field, are supposed to receive 15 days of free C rations per month. Why was this recently cut down to 7 or 8 days per month?
4. A certain number of wounded soldiers in the field lost their lives because they were not evacuated to the hospital in time. Why was that?

Questions 1 and 2, I invited my superior to answer the next day. [With regard to question 3,] I said the stocks have dwindled that were left behind by the U.S. forces. Beginning one year before the fall of Vietnam, the C rations were "money in hand" for the commander. When the commander needed something—for his unit or his private purpose—his headquarters company used the C rations. [With regard to question 4,] I said I don't know exactly the percentage of wounded soldiers who died because of lack of medical evacuation. I don't have any statistics, but I'm sure there were many.

Colonel Thuc said he then made valiant efforts to give cogent explanations for this last circumstance, primarily on the grounds of technical and terrain problems. He then outlined the principal complaints of soldiers voiced during his sessions: "The first related to clothing, salary and medicines. The second related to complaints by soldiers who had not received any annual leave after 12 months in the field, including emergency leave. The third related to spoiled C rations." The soldiers, it seems, were quite interested in the military situation and the operations they were called upon to conduct. Colonel Thuc reported that he discussed impending operations with his soldiers in detail, and that subsequently they took pride in executing what they "had planned with their boss." It is known that the enemy made extensive use of this practice (in the form of sandbox exercises), apparently with good success. The extent to which other commanders followed Colonel Thuc's practice as a morale booster did not emerge from what the respondents said.

Apparently the South Vietnamese Army, unlike the enemy, did not have morale redressing and maintaining systems such as the three-man cell or the Khiem Tao (Criticism/Self-Criticism) which were practiced across the board by the North Vietnamese, seemingly with great effect. Respondents had little to say on the subject of enemy morale. Some considered it good, but others added their version of "the enemy was not ten feet tall." One prominent division commander said that the enemy soldiers, once captured, were just bedraggled and underage boys. "But while in the system they were different and very effective."[17]

Despite these discouraging factors, which also include a catastrophic financial situation due to galloping inflation that forced South Vietnamese soldiers to hustle and moonlight to feed their families, ARVN morale was reported to be remarkably high in some places, at some times, and in some units. This seems confirmed by the fighting they did during the enemy offensive of 1972 and during the bloody fighting in 1973 and 1974. ARVN soldiers are reported to have fought heroically at An Loc in 1972 and in ARVN's last battle, at Xuan Loc, in 1975. Respondents stated that during inspection tours in 1974 they saw many soldiers evincing very high morale, and that in 1975 many soldiers were ready to fight and were bitterly disappointed that they did not get an opportunity to confront the enemy. Some, according to an artillery colonel, "pleaded with tears in their eyes for a chance to fight."

The Collapse of Morale

Yet, like everything else in South Vietnam, under the impact of the final enemy offensive in 1975 the soldiers' morale also collapsed. In brief, from what the respondents reported, three factors were primarily responsible for this collapse.

First, there was what the last Prime Minister, Nguyen Ba Can, called the complete "psychological collapse" that hit everyone in

---

[17] In all, this report contains very little about what respondents thought about the enemy soldiers. They talked very little about them. Overall, they attributed the collapse of South Vietnam more to the weaknesses in their own camp than to the strength in the enemy's. However, none of the respondents discounted the enemy soldier or his morale in any way.

South Vietnam, from Thieu on down to the last soldier and civilian, because "the war had lasted too long, had been too costly, and had offered too few prospects of favorable termination."

The second factor, stressed particularly by Marshal Ky but also by others, was that the commanders, whether on Thieu's orders or on their own, had allegedly refused to fight and had in fact abandoned their units in many cases.

And third, there was the belief spread by rumors that "deals" had been made to abandon new areas of South Vietnam to the Communists or that the advancing enemy would soon swamp the areas where the soldiers' families lived. At that point many soldiers apparently deserted, perhaps not so much to save their own lives as to save those of their families, who were now endangered by an enemy who was only too well remembered for what he had done at Hue during the Tet offensive in 1968.[18]

One observer summarized the collapse of morale by declaring that it had been undermined by South Vietnam's history of political instability, coups, and the frustrations of war, along with the inflation that had particularly affected the morale of junior officers, NCOs, and soldiers, many of whom were living at bare subsistence levels. Therefore, he said, the collapse was "really not all that sudden." What had perhaps been most demoralizing of all was, as one respondent put it, "everyone's conviction that the enemy would never give up."

[18] These desertions may confirm the view of some of the respondents that the American way of seeing and conducting the war and of training ARVN in their image was not well suited to the war in Vietnam. But it was not so much the American tendency to think in terms of conventional war that clashed with the realities of the situation. Rather, the U.S. fighting doctrines and methods were designed for fighting wars abroad, not at home amidst one's own civilian population. Apparently, this factor had not been considered by anybody except the enemy, who was presumably fully cognizant of the hazards for ARVN (and the opportunities for himself) of fighting in-country. American concern for the morale of the fighting man centers around treatment, weapons, rotation, support, R&R, and similar considerations, but it does not include his family, which is assumed to be living safely at home while he fights abroad. Just as the intense use of the firepower in-country proved to be counterproductive, in the opinion of some respondents, the presence of soldiers' families in contested areas proved to be a fatal morale hazard for ARVN troops.

Chapter 7

The Balance of Forces Before the 1975 Offensive

The Balance of Forces Before the 1975 Offensive

In the minds of most of the South Vietnamese respondents, the balance of military forces was much to their disadvantage at the beginning of 1975. Buu Vien said:

> When the Communists decided on waging their final war against the Republic of Vietnam in the spring of 1975, they knew, and the rest of the world knew, that their military forces were by far stronger than those of South Vietnam.

Armed Forces Strength

On paper, ARVN had eleven infantry divisions, one marine and one airborne division, some Ranger forces and armored units, and a considerable number of Regional and Popular Forces. All this added up, on paper, to 1.1 million men under arms. Compared to that, intelligence estimates were that the enemy had more than a dozen divisions plus special units (engineers, antiaircraft) in the South and up to seven reserve divisions in the North. Buu Vien commented:

> At the time the cease-fire was signed in 1973, there was an estimated force of 300,000 North Vietnamese troops in South Vietnam, besides the local troops belonging to the National Liberation Front . . . the 300,000 never went back to North Vietnam. On the

contrary, by systematically violating the cease-fire agreement, the [enemy] quietly infiltrated more of their troops into South Vietnam. The exact figure is not known, but it could not have been under the 100,000 mark. By the time of South Vietnam's final collapse, Saigon alone was surrounded by 17 NVA divisions.

Even though there may not have been too great a discrepancy between the respective forces of the two sides on the simple basis of numbers (even with such massive infiltration and invasion, the enemy had fewer troops in South Vietnam than ARVN), the balance appears to have been in favor of the enemy, since presumably, the enemy's troops had a very high ratio of actual combat soldiers among them, whereas ARVN not only had a considerable "tail," but its effective strength also was reported to be far below the official strength figure due to the ghost soldiers and the continuing high desertion rate. When asked what the actual effective combat strength of ARVN was at the time, General Tran Van Don replied:

A. It will surprise you to learn exactly how many fighters [ARVN actually had]. One hundred thousand. I don't call them fighters when they belong to the logistical units.

Q. You had a one-million-man army but only one hundred thousand fighters?

A. Yes.

The comparative weakness of ARVN becomes even more apparent in view of the radical difference between its mission and that of the enemy: Whereas ARVN was spread extremely thin in accordance with the defensive strategy still prevailing on the eve of the big offensive, the enemy was free to concentrate his forces and attack at will. He was doubly free to do so, as ARVN did not have the capability to interfere with North Vietnam's massive staging activities along South Vietnam's western borders.

One senior combat general in the northern sector reported that a Communist document captured in 1972 stated that "Saigon's infantry + American Fire Power = National Liberation Front's Army." The general, agreeing with this formula, added, "In this rough equation, if one were to take out the American firepower, we can immediately see the results." Subsequently, when discussing the battle of An Loc in 1972, where valiant fighting by ARVN, supported by American B-52s, defeated the enemy, the general established his own formula: "Saigon's infantry + American Fire Power > NLF's Army." What the general tried to emphasize here is what virtually all the respondents emphasized, that in their estimation the containment of the 1972 enemy offensive was mainly due to the B-52s; most respondents seemed to think that the 1975 offensive could also have been contained had B-52s been available.

It is not clear, however, precisely what the respondents felt could have alleviated ARVN's manpower shortage. While ARVN had no mobile reserves, the enemy had as many as seven reserve divisions that could be committed from the North. One senior JGS officer reported that from 1969 on, the United States had been asked many times to support the activation of additional combat divisions in South Vietnam but had "never satisfied" these requests. The respondent said that MACV had turned down these requests on the grounds of cost and instead had argued that it was better for the GVN to build up the less-expensive Regional and Popular Forces. When asked to speculate on why he thought MACV had taken this position, this officer said it stemmed from the separation of missions which had existed in Vietnam during the American presence. According to the American concept, it was the U.S. mission to fight Communist main force units, while ARVN's task was primarily to provide territorial security for Pacification. He went on to state that the buildup of a fourth brigade for both the Airborne and Marine Divisions was accomplished out of equipment stores that the GVN already had on hand, and once this was accomplished there were no additional replacements. Thus, it was impossible to create additional reserve divisions without U.S. support. On the other hand, according to manpower expert Buu Vien, it did not seem possible to draft even more men than ARVN already had, or, under prevailing man-

133

power policies, to stem the widespread desertions. Perhaps the ARVN force posture could have been drastically changed, as some of the more enterprising colonels suggested, to create a large mobile strike force or, alternatively, through the adoption of the "people's army" concept as advocated by Tran Van Don.

Whether or not any of the changes proposed in hindsight (or at the time) would have been possible, they did not take place, and as a result ARVN was clearly inferior in "foxhole strength" when the big push came, according to the respondents.

Even if the regular infantry divisions had not been under-strength, their defensive missions were, in the view of the respondents, far too large for them. Estimates of the additional forces required ranged from three to six divisions. This requirement for additional forces seemed to be especially true of II Corps, which had only two infantry divisions for its defense, the 22nd and 23rd, thereby making the strategically vital central highlands a most inviting target for the enemy, who did in fact launch his offensive there. According to its Chief of Staff, II Corps would have needed at least another one to two divisions. But even the five-division force defending I Corps, in the view of its Commander, General Truong, was also spread too thin and was in need of at least two additional divisions, even if the enemy did not commit any of his reserve divisions held in the North.

The insufficient number of divisions is another example of the vicious circles in which the South Vietnamese leaders, according to their testimony, were caught. On the one hand, additional divisions could not be raised because of the many different man-power problems that existed. On the other, the activation of new divisions, even if the manpower problems could have been solved, was described as not possible because equipment was lacking due to U.S. aid reductions and also because of the American coolness to the idea when it was discussed in earlier years.

The Enemy Buildup

While ARVN, according to the respondents, was facing big manpower problems in its final battles with the enemy, its logistic problems were, if anything, even greater. Two obverse trends had taken place since the Paris Agreements: The enemy's logistical position had greatly improved, while ARVN's had greatly deteriorated. Colonel Do Ngoc Nhan, a JGS officer, said:

Let's read the report from the South Vietnam Central Intelligence Organization to the South Vietnamese military delegation in late 1974: "While the U.S. has reduced its aid to South Vietnam, the Soviet Union had doubled its assistance to North Vietnam to 1.5 billion dollars. The Communists have used 30,000 prisoners released by South Vietnam to reinforce their units. At the same time, about 100,000 cadres and soldiers have infiltrated South Vietnam using the Ho Chi Minh Trail and the DMZ. With regard to heavy weapons, the Communists have sent to South Vietnam about 600 tanks, 500 heavy cannons, 200 antiaircraft weapons and many SA-7 rockets in addition to what they had. The Communist force has been reorganized on a large scale, now comprising 17 combat divisions, excluding 40,000 North Vietnamese troops in Cambodia and 50,000 troops in Laos. Every week, on the expanded Ho Chi Minh Trail, 1500 trucks were moved day and night. Their pipeline system constructed to supply gas is now only 80 kilometers from Saigon.

Another high-ranking officer made these observations:

Air photos also showed unusual activities in Dong Ha which had become [North Vietnam's] main logistical center, where supplies were brought in from Hanoi by trucks moving down on Highway 1 and also by Navy and commercial ships through the strategic port of Cua Viet that we failed to secure. The supply by sea, in fact, had become more important after the Paris Agreements. Air reconnaissance had detected a daily average of 10 Hong Ky (Red flag) ships of Red China going through Cua Viet.

Clearly, the enemy's road-building and pipeline-laying activities were among the most important parts of the buildup. The old Ho Chi Minh Trail was apparently no longer adequate to bring down the increased supplies, so the enemy constructed what came to be known among ARVN officers as "Ho Chi Minh East," a

135

modern network of roads. This new road network, which was built at the same time that supplies were being brought south, not only multiplied the amount of infiltration traffic but—perhaps even more importantly—dramatically cut the time required to bring men and materiel down, from several months to a matter of days, according to some respondents:

One general said:

> The Communists (after Paris) began to build a sophisticated net of routes across mountains and creeks to bring supplies all the way to MR III around Saigon. Their engineer units worked feverishly day and night to cut roads through forests and hills. Every day one could hear echoes of detonations beyond the range of mountains to the west of Highway 1. In fact, to build more roads and to speed up the flow of supplies to the South, three engineer and transportation divisions were activated. These divisions were under direct control of NVA High Command and were comprised of four engineer and four transportation regiments each. Not content with the old Ho Chi Minh Trail on the Laotian border, they had built a new road east of the Annamite Mountains, running parallel to our Highway 1. This new road, sometimes called "Ho Chi Minh East," permitted the supplies to be brought directly to their troops in the front line. Besides these two roads running southward, they had also built or repaired a sophisticated system of lateral roads which permitted them to bypass and to envelop every one of our big cities. These included in MR I, just to name a few, the important road which ran from A Shau Valley to the strategic area of Truoi, south of Hue, and all the way south of Hai Van Pass through the Col de Bay; and also the road which linked the Ho Chi Minh Trail to Bengiang and Thuong Duc District town, southwest of Danang and to the already mentioned Que Son Valley.

But the Communist buildup included much more. The general continued:

> A system of pipelines was also installed along these roads to provide POL for their mechanized units operating in the South. Dong Ha and Khe Sanh airfields were repaired, and in order to provide protection to these strategic bases, they established around

them an interlocking system of antiaircraft weapons. It is significant to note that in Quang Tri province alone, the North Vietnamese Army had eight antiaircraft regiments whose armaments ranged all the way from 12.7-mm machine guns to SAM missiles. In the last months of 1974, the Communists dramatically increased their logistical activities. Our air reconnaissances detected convoys of hundreds of Molotova trucks moving south, day and night, in the area northwest of Pleiku and southwest of Danang. Despite heavy losses inflicted by our airstrikes, they kept moving. In the region northwest of Kontum, in February 1975, South Vietnamese Air Force armed reconnaissance detected a convoy of around 400 trucks and reportedly destroyed over 200. These figures might have been inflated, nonetheless they can give an idea of the dramatic improvement in North Vietnam's logistical capabilities. It was estimated that in MR I alone, in 1974, over 10,000 tons of supplies (mostly ammunition and food) were infiltrated every month. The Communists had brought into South Vietnam from the moment the Paris Agreements went into effect until the end of 1975 a large quantity of heavy equipment consisting of 1,000 tanks of all types, and more than 600 field artillery pieces. The new weapons and military supplies included improved SA-7 rockets, T-34 tanks with portable bridges, 152-mm cannons, and M-2 personnel carriers towing artillery.

The ARVN "Build-Down"

Thus, the enemy effected a buildup after the Paris Agreements that was not only vast in extent but impressive in its multifaceted nature and in the efficiency and integration of its utilization. In the first place, external Communist aid, according to the respondents, increased greatly in quantity and improved greatly in quality. Second, the enemy dramatically improved his ability to move supplies and soldiers to where they were needed. Third, he greatly increased his mobility for the battles to come by his new roads and pipeline system. Fourth, he strengthened his air defenses to a point where the entire system became virtually invulnerable. Besides, as all respondents agreed, he had greatly improved his proficiency in using his equipment, especially armor. Finally, the enemy had immensely improved his strategic position by building a network of lateral roads leading from Ho Chi Minh East in a westerly direction toward the sea, so that he could prevent ARVN from moving up supplies or withdrawing troops, and could effectively bottle up ARVN units and fleeing civilians at will.

By contrast, ARVN's logistical problems had greatly intensified. These problems were of two quite different types: One was insufficient or inadequate hardware, and the other was poor administration of that hardware.

The primary source of information on the subject of the supplies themselves was Colonel Pham Ky Loan, Deputy Commander of the Central Logistics Command. Colonel Loan began by saying:

> After the Paris Agreements we realized that supplies were going to decline. In the first year, aid was still 1.4 billion. But starting with the next fiscal year it was cut down to half. So at CLC [the Central Logistics Command] we tried to submit our recommendations and suggestions to all branches about savings, to try to have everybody make better use of what we had. Our principal emphasis was on ammunition, because from 70 to 80 percent of the funds were used for that.
>
> Ammunition was running short. As you know, in our situation, beginning 1974, the rate of incidents everywhere in the country rose sharply, mostly—and you may not be aware of that—in the Delta area, so that the need for ammunition was very great. These small outposts, when attacked, needed lots of artillery support.
>
> The second shortage, right after the ammunition shortage in importance, was the shortage of fuel. For the choppers, the fighters, ships and trucks. It cut the operational hours in half. This did not happen right after the American withdrawal. It declined gradually, until it was down to half in 1974.
>
> I discussed this at every one of our weekly meetings with the Defense Attaché and General Khuyen. They were all aware of it. The Americans said they would try their best, but on their side they were limited by the available funds. I recognize their efforts, but they had their ceiling and there was nothing they could do about it.

Colonel Loan continued:

One big trouble we had was spare parts. Mostly for planes. For example, the transport aircraft we had was the old C-130A. The Americans no longer use the C-130As. So it was really hard to get all the spare parts for this old model. We had thirty C-130s, but the average daily number we could actually use—and I know this very well because I controlled them—was five. Five planes out of two squadrons of thirty! The spare parts would eventually be supplied, but as they were not in manufacture anymore it took a long time to make them. So, most of the C-130s were grounded most of the time.

Anyway, we tried to stretch what we had and spend it as wisely as we could. As you know, all our requests had to go through the Defense Attaché's Office for screening. Most of the time he okayed our requests. But even so, we often did not get supplies on time. The request would go to Okinawa or some other place.

To repeat: In the beginning the trouble was with spare parts, ammunition, POL. I personally headed a lecture team that went to every Corps command in 1974. The lectures were to be attended by the Corps commander and his deputy and all high-ranking officers, to tell them how tight the situation was and what to do to save ammunition, etc. But whatever system we advocated, it created big problems for the field commanders. As for their ASR (Average Supply Rate), we generally gave them half of what they asked for—this created big problems for them. Of course, it really created two problems: a tactical problem, and a morale problem for the troops, who don't like to fight with insufficient ammunition. This was aggravated by the lack of fuel which cut down the flying hours of the planes so that the field units relied even more heavily on artillery support.[19]

[19] According to one deputy Corps commander, this was the situation in his area:

Weapon	Average Supply Rate	
Caliber	1972	1975
105	180	10
155	150	5
175	30	3

Colonel Loan proceeded:

> What was particularly aggravating was that the monthly allocation
> of ammo was exhausted around the 25th of the month. And the
> enemy knew this, of course, and took advantage of it. . . . Take
> the M-16. Soldiers going into combat regularly receive 400 rounds.
> But with the ammo shortage this had to be cut down to 200. That
> reduced his fighting capability and his morale. Particularly because
> we had trained our soldiers to conduct the war American style. As a
> result, every soldier confronted with the enemy requested air sup-
> port and/or artillery support. In addition, our air transport became
> increasingly restricted. We thus lost our greatest advantage over
> the enemy: mobility and firepower. So soldiers had to walk—it was
> the only way. And they didn't like that, for sure. Meanwhile, the
> other side knew [all] that and they had more favorable conditions
> than in the past.

Colonel Loan continued his catalog of problems:

> In order to preserve ammunition, and money, we eliminated in
> 1974 everything except HE. [We did without] flares, illuminating
> shells, etc. They cost too much money. We could no longer afford
> to shoot illuminating flares. The POL shortage was mostly of GP4,
> used for choppers and fighter planes. With regard to spare parts, the
> hardest hit, aside from the C-130s, were the choppers, the
> Chinooks. Then there was a bad shortage of artillery tubes, spare
> parts for APCs, M-16 barrels. We had to use the old 3.5 rocket
> launcher instead of LAWs as an antitank weapon. Those 3.5s were
> WW-II weapons, you should be aware of that. You can see them in
> all the movies [laughter].

The enemy, according to Loan, knew what was going on:

> The North Vietnamese were definitely aware of our strapped situa-
> tion. They knew about the troubles we had with military aid. We
> were not able to rebuild the battle-damaged APCs or the M-48
> tanks. We had to send them to the States to rebuild them. But the
> U.S. depot required the BIIL—the Basic Issues Items List—that
> means all auxiliary equipment that comes with the main item, such

as radio equipment or gun mounts. We tried our best to send along these BIILs, but most of the time the pieces had been lost in combat. When they rebuilt the basic items they sent [them] back to us without BIILs. So we might get a rebuilt tank without radio. Also, it took a very long time to ship the equipment to the U.S. and get it back. Months and months. There were not enough ships coming to Vietnam.

Loan then mentioned Navy supplies:

I was in charge of supplies for the Navy, too. The Navy was also in bad shape from the point of view of supplies. The worst was that they lost the mobility of their small craft that had been very useful to patrol on the rivers. They were short of fuel, spare parts, too. Ammunition was okay, because their needs were limited. But POL and spare parts were bad.

Besides, said Loan, while some U.S. equipment was obsolete, other equipment was too sophisticated:

The M-48 tank, for example. The firing devices. You could count on your fingers the men who could expertly repair them. Mostly these tanks had to be sent back to the U.S. for repair. We had some U.S. advisers and Filipino repairmen, but they did not help much. Even the M-16 rifle. Do you know that you had to use three different types of oil to grease them? If you compare that with the AK47! Much simpler to maintain, and very good for firing. And then there was some equipment that we really did not need. For example, the 8-inch gun. We had three battalions of these. They were much too big. That gun could fire 30 kilometers, but we never knew whether it hit the target or not. Just "firing blind." Maybe the Americans just left it in Vietnam because they did not want to move such heavy equipment back to the U.S. Then the TOW missile. Too expensive—one cost $3000. And it did not do much good in killing enemy tanks.

But didn't the enemy have some quite sophisticated equipment, too?

141

Well, the SAM-7 was quite simple. And their heat-seeking devices were very simple. The TOW just wasn't right for our troops. The best was the M72, one of your best weapons, and that we ran out of. They were good antitank weapons. The 105 and 155 were very good weapons. The enemy had still better weapons, though. One weapon our troops were most scared of was the 130. It can fire farther than the 105s, is very accurate and devastating in the impact area. The enemy began using them in 1972.

Loan then made several general remarks:

U.S. aid should have been *consistent*. Supporting a one-million-man army and having to fight the enemy continuously, we had to worry all the time about money. We were never sure what we would get or how much—how could we plan? I think President Thieu made the point to President Nixon when he saw him at San Clemente, to have a three-year military aid program amounting to $3 or 4 billion, a long-term commitment. But you could not give such a commitment because of your internal policy, the Congress, the American public. Consistency would also have helped our morale.[20] And one more thing: [You] should have been more patient. The enemy is very patient. So are we (South Vietnam). That's why we were able to fight against the Communists for over thirty years. Unfortunately our allies did not share the same idea. One more thing: The POL shortage affected the operation time of the choppers, so we could not use them to evacuate all the wounded. That was really bad.

Colonel Loan then concluded with some striking figures:

I have some figures here. The U.S. spent $150 billion on the war. But we spent only about one and a half million dollars a day on

---

[20] In this connection, one general pointed to the differences in U.S. military aid in different areas. He said ". . . for the fiscal year South Vietnam got $300 million in military aid, out of $700 million which had been appropriated by Congress. It is significant . . . that Israel got $2.1 billion in military aid during the three-week Middle East War in 1973; in other words, South Vietnam in one year got $1/7$th of what Israel got in 3 weeks." By contrast, said Colonel Loan, "Russian aid for North Vietnam in 1975 was over $1 billion." How did he know? "It's just a guess."

ARVN after 1972. That is very little if you consider that you were supporting a force of one million men. *It is hardly more than one dollar a day per man.* Not enough. Especially if that force is equipped just like the U.S., as far as weapons and materiel is concerned. In 1974, when aid went down by 50 percent, incidents went up, they almost doubled. At that time over 50 percent of the aid went for ammo. But the decline in the dollar amount for ammo did not reflect the actual decline. The actual decline was much greater, because in 1974 the price of brass went up by about 20 percent.[21]

On the broad issue of whether the outcome might have been different if South Vietnam had had what he would regard as sufficient materiel, Loan said, "I think we could have held South Vietnam indefinitely." And even with the supply shortages that plagued him for years he felt that on the basis of an inspection trip a few weeks before the fall of Ban Me Thuot, "we were in good shape (there), we had enough supplies to defend the area." But when assessing the balance of forces throughout the theater at the time the last big enemy offensive began, the materiel situation as it actually was, on the basis of Loan's description, was a big minus item in the equation.

Artillery

After the Paris Agreements, ARVN artillery was greatly plagued by being pulled in two opposite directions. On the one hand, ARVN, spoiled by lavish American fire support even when confronted with only a few snipers, was now left without it and expected ARVN artillery to take up the slack. But at the same time, ammunition stocks declined and orders were given to preserve ammunition. In fact, quota systems were established, which President Thieu—at least in some official meetings—personally opposed "angrily," on the ground that the soldiers should get their ammunition according to need, not quota. However, in the field,

---

[21] The worst blow, however, was the enormous increase in the price of oil, according to several respondents.

the quota system was observed to some extent, apparently with adverse consequences on the effectiveness of the artillery, the morale of artillery soldiers, and the morale of the soldiers of infantry units the artillery was supposed to protect. "While in 1972 we could shoot an unlimited number of artillery rounds (provided that the rate of fire was not too fast to damage the bore of the tube)," wrote one commander, "in 1975 the average available supply rate (ASR) was less than 10 percent of what we fired in 1972."[22]

General Thinh, Commanding General of the Artillery Command, said that the ground commanders were always complaining about reduction of support missions by the Air Force, and the conclusion generally was that artillery should be used instead. But even when sufficient shells were available to step up artillery activity, this was against JGS directives. In order to relieve insufficient artillery support, some infantry units then tried using their mortars more than before, only to discover that mortar shells were even more restricted.

It is well known, and was widely displayed on television, that vast stocks of ammunition and other supplies eventually fell into enemy hands in 1975. The respondents saw no contradiction between this and their claim that stocks were insufficient. Their reasoning was that these stocks were reserves which could not be used up as long as the war was expected to go on. In fact, conflicts arose toward the end between some field commanders who wanted to use all available stocks in "go-for-broke" fashion and logistics personnel who wanted to keep observing the quota system and to hold stocks in reserve.

At the same time, the enemy artillery was said to have been very effective, especially the Russian 130. Though its range was, at 27 km, 5 km less than that of the big American 175, it was simpler and more manageable and was used to good advantage by the enemy. However, according to witnesses, the enemy artillerists were no supermen and were not necessarily better than their ARVN counterparts. The reasons for the tremendous difference in effect were

[22] Actually, some other respondents reported that the reductions, though drastic, were not quite that severe.

in the nature of the war: ARVN had very few lucrative targets (only enemy positions) and had great difficulty in acquiring them, but for the enemy, South Vietnam was just a mass of lucrative targets—almost everything from buildings to depots, from storage tanks to airfields, from headquarters to civilian installations. Finally, under JGS pressure, ARVN artillery had been reorganized to some extent in 1974, to the detriment of efficiency, according to its commander.

As regards specific operations, a high-ranking artillery officer reported that sensors did not appreciably enhance ARVN capabilities—on the contrary:

> Thanks to captured enemy soldiers, we learned that the enemy was well aware of our [use of sensors]. Every time enemy troops found our sensors dropped to the ground by air, they picked them up, but instead of destroying them they left them in open fields with branches and trees . . . around them. At night, strong winds blowing through the open fields would rattle the leaves of those branches . . . and produce effects upon the sensors which would be picked up in the central station as information, and thus caused us to waste our ammunition.

Overall, according to the respondents, ARVN artillery also suffered from the same affliction that plagued the other ARVN services: uncertainties as to doctrine and tactics. Organization on the U.S. pattern, according to the high-ranking artillery officer, was a mistake in the first place. It geared the artillery for conventional war, which was not then taking place, and it also made the artillery unsuitable for the existing terrain. He elaborated as follows:

> With my experience during my adolescent years, living in Communist-controlled areas, and with the experiences I had gained through participation in the 1950 to 1954 war in North Vietnam, I was certain that we would [not] encounter a conventional type of war such as the American Advisory Groups, from TRIM to MAAG, shaped ARVN to fight. At that time, I raised those questions for discussion with the U.S. advisers in my unit. They

answered, "We are adopting modern methods of training and organization which have been carefully appraised by high-echelon staff commands, and cannot be erroneous." They told me to be confident and strive to get more good results (in war fighting) as I had done in the past.

Then, when what amounted to conventional war finally came, ammunition was short and mobility restricted.

Respondents on the whole seemed to agree that in the balance of forces, the ARVN artillery did not have an edge over that of the enemy. In fact, because the North Vietnamese had greater mobility, and because of the nature of the war, the enemy artillery had the advantage, according to two senior artillery officers, including General Thinh.

The South Vietnamese Air Force

Having an air force of more than a thousand aircraft might have been expected to weigh considerably in ARVN's favor in the balance of forces, but according to the respondents, this was not the case. One reason for this was that all of them considered "airpower" to mean primarily B-52s and (to a far lesser extent) F-4s, i.e., planes they did not have. As already stated, most respondents credited the B-52s with having played a decisive part in their containment of the 1972 enemy offensive, and most believed that the 1975 enemy offensive might have had a similiar fate if B-52s had been available, particularly in view of the enemy's tactic of moving and assembling his forces in broad daylight —a practice, they say, he could not have employed had B-52s been used.

The apparent lack of efficacy of VNAF was not always attributed to the same factors, however. Different respondents stressed different disabilities.

A high-ranking VNAF officer—a man originally trained as an artillery officer, who later joined the Air Force and was appointed to his post by Nguyen Cao Ky—stated that the air forces were hampered by the fact that command over the aircraft was in the hands of the Corps commanders. He stressed the fact that "our mission remained basically unchanged: to support the ground forces." This means, in plainer terms, that when ARVN failed to do its job of stopping the enemy, VNAF was in no position to do so. But there were also big problems of command and control. He added:

> In any battle, the Air Force always supported the ground forces. But the concentration of fire was decided not by the Air Force, but by the JGS, because they were the ones who allocated . . . the amount of sorties and ammunition. They did this by allocating planes to each Corps. The Air Force did not have the authority to determine the number of sorties or the expenditure of ammunition without the permission of the Corps commanders.

As for the value of the aircraft at VNAF's disposal, this same officer stated:

> The F-5 is a very good aircraft and the pilots liked to fly it. But it was not suitable. It is a very nice plane, but the load is not big enough, and the autonomy of the aircraft is insufficient—it can fly only one hour and fifteen minutes. We would have needed B-52s that could release their loads beyond the range of the SAM-7. Still, with the help of our American counterparts we developed techniques for high-altitude release.

Were these techniques attaining accuracy?

> Not so accurate. It is very hard to get accuracy from high altitudes.

The problem of attaining accuracy in bombing from high altitudes had, according to various respondents, two related components: On the one hand, the enemy had excellent antiaircraft defenses and was also favored by the terrain in that he could often place his defenses on mountain ridges, thereby increasing their range, while his forces operated in the valleys. On the other hand, there was a morale problem in that flying low enough to increase accuracy in the face of such defenses required the pilots to be willing to take great risks. This willingness, according to some field commanders who deplored the absence of effective air support, was often lacking.

This question was raised with Marshal Ky:

Q. Were losses of aircraft a lot heavier in 1975?

A. Not really heavier because, at the end, now, that is, I'm very frank, most of the pilots didn't take too much risk, so they drop their bombs from very high. . . .

Q. That's what we have heard from your field commanders. Several of them complained about VNAF for that reason. Are these complaints justified?

A. Oh yes, I'm sure. Because the pilots came back and told me. Why risk my life with that regime (in Saigon)? If I die, what for? So, you know. . . .

Q. Their morale had really declined?

A. Exactly. . . . That's something that never happened when I was Commander of the Air Force. But at the end, a squadron leader of the 837th came to me and said to me, "Frankly," he said, "you know, now I drop a bomb at 35,000 feet because I don't want to go down and be hit by Communist antiaircraft. What for?"

Ky also attributed part of this low pilot morale to the financial distress under which the pilots lived.

Colonel Vu Van Uoc, VNAF's Chief Operations Officer, commented on the vulnerability of the planes:

The majority of the VNAF planes were built 10, 15, sometimes even 30 years ago—except for the A-37s remade from the T-37s, and the F-5Es. These old planes were very slow compared to the firing capabilities of enemy antiaircraft, especially their SA-7 missiles and big caliber cannon capable of shooting down planes flying at over 18,000 feet. . . . In other words, our Air Force was a very easy target for the North Vietnamese during the years

148

1973–1975. For these latter had assembled too many antiaircraft guns along with ground-to-air missiles on every battlefield.

Uoc also pointed to the fact that the Communists had changed their tactics toward the end of the war and moved in so quickly when attacking a town that VNAF had difficulty operating against them.

The next factor, mentioned by a high-ranking VNAF officer, was VNAF leadership:

> . . . In my Air Force most of the wing commanders did not like their superiors at all because they were unqualified to be commanders. But Thieu put them in as commanders because they [obeyed] Thieu. The wing commanders did not like the men at headquarters. They don't like Minh (Commanding General of VNAF), and I don't like Minh. From the military point of view, he was not qualified. And his deputy chief for operations, the same! How can they command the air divisions and the wing commanders? They don't know . . . how to fight a battle! How can they give orders?

This officer also complained that the Americans did not teach them enough of the required skills:

> The American Air Force trained the Vietnamese only in how to use American planes. How to fight the supply arteries, the LOCs and release the bombs, that's all. As for tactics and strategy, we never had a chance to learn them, except some of the F-5E pilots. We just had to learn ourselves in the field. So we benefited from the American force through the U.S. advisers only in technical matters—how to repair planes with the system used by the USAF. Supply, that's all. Battlefield—we learned nothing from them.[23]

Then, aside from the general problems that plagued VNAF, such as the shortage of POL and spares, two more problems were

---

[23] At this point in the interview, apparently reliving his frustrations, the officer exclaimed, "The American people do not understand the oriental society! That's the problem. You put in Thieu, you put in Diem, you let Diem be killed, you kick out everybody, you lose again! You want them to listen to you but you didn't want to listen to them!"

mentioned. One was that ground-air communications allegedly were poor, so that support of ground operations was difficult. The other was that, particularly toward the end of the war, ARVN was unable to protect the airfields sufficiently to permit effective VNAF operations.

The Chief Operations Officer of VNAF expressed this view: "Had our airbases been securely protected, it is certain that the war would have been prolonged and the issue been very much in the balance . . . the Air Forces did not have the opportunity to destroy the enemy because our bases were harassed by enemy rockets, mortar, and artillery. . . . Helicopters are no good for troop transport in a guerrilla war. And if you take 130s, every time you land or take off they attack the airbase with rockets. The ground troops cannot give you good protection of the airbase—you need control at least up to 20 miles away from the base. The ground forces did not have the strength to protect the airbases so the Air Force could not perform its mission. That was the problem."

Thus, if we can believe the respondents, VNAF, on the whole, was not the instrument to tip the balance of forces into South Vietnam's favor, even though the enemy did not have any planes at all in the South.

The Bottom Line

All the respondent statements presented to this point indicate that the Vietnamese military leaders regarded the balance of forces in 1974–1975 to be unfavorable to them in every respect. This included the psychological aspects: The South Vietnamese felt that U.S. interest in their cause had waned greatly, whereas the enemy's support from the Communist world continued unabated.

The enemy, it seems, shared this assessment and therefore felt ready to attack. In particular, the North Vietnamese apparently viewed their new lines of communication as their most valuable asset. Self-serving though the words of General Van Tien Dung, Commander-in-Chief of the North Vietnamese forces in the South, may be, their vivid imagery conveys this quite well:

Our old and new communication lines (highways and pipeline) resembled endless lengths of sturdy hemp ropes being daily and hourly slipped around the neck and limbs of the monster who would be strangled with one sharp yank when the order was given.[24]

Thus, the stage was set at the beginning of 1975 for a military campaign that—as we now know—brought greater and faster results to the North Vietnamese than even they had anticipated.

[24] Van Tien Dung, *Great Spring Victory*, op. cit., p. 3.

PART II
The Collapse

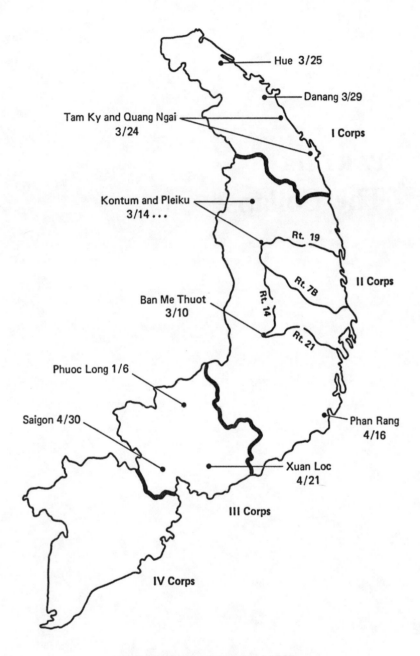

Hue 3/25

Danang 3/29

Tam Ky and Quang Ngai
3/24

I Corps

Kontum and Pleiku
3/14 . . .

Rt. 19

Rt. 7B

Rt. 14

II Corps

Ban Me Thuot
3/10

Rt. 21

Phuoc Long 1/6

Saigon 4/30

Phan Rang
4/16

Xuan Loc
4/21

III Corps

IV Corps

THE SEQUENCE OF THE COLLAPSE

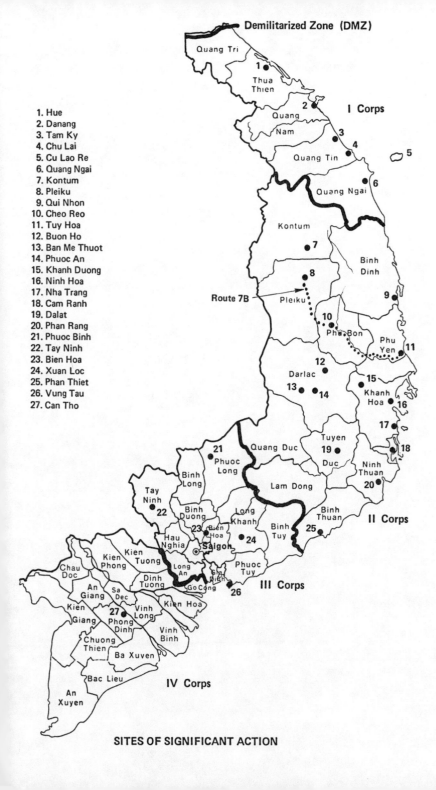

Demilitarized Zone (DMZ)

1. Hue
2. Danang
3. Tam Ky
4. Chu Lai
5. Cu Lao Re
6. Quang Ngai
7. Kontum
8. Pleiku
9. Qui Nhon
10. Cheo Reo
11. Tuy Hoa
12. Buon Ho
13. Ban Me Thuot
14. Phuoc An
15. Khanh Duong
16. Ninh Hoa
17. Nha Trang
18. Cam Ranh
19. Dalat
20. Phan Rang
21. Phuoc Binh
22. Tay Ninh
23. Bien Hoa
24. Xuan Loc
25. Phan Thiet
26. Vung Tau
27. Can Tho

I Corps

II Corps

III Corps

IV Corps

Route 7B

SITES OF SIGNIFICANT ACTION

Chapter 8

The Beginning of the End: The Loss of Phuoc Long

The Beginning of the End:
The Loss of Phuoc Long

In the view of one former senior ARVN general, the collapse of South Vietnam "was nothing but a succession of successful envelopments."

> . . . Communist strategy, very simple in nature, had not really changed in 1975, but the execution had been made easier and more effective, thanks to the new sophisticated net of roads. This strategy could be called "a strategy of indirect approach" if we were to use Liddell Hart's terminology. It consisted of making a frontal attack with a relatively small force to [fix] ARVN units, while executing a deep envelopment in the rear to isolate the big cities and cut off the main lines of communication.

By applying military pressure in all four Corps areas simultaneously, Hanoi was able to exploit an overextended and static GVN defensive posture that, for a variety of reasons, apparently was far too brittle to cope with anything like a multifront attack. Summing up the nature of this military problem, and the GVN's strategic weaknesses, another former general officer stated:

> The Communist offensive in late 1974 and early 1975 was launched simultaneously in all the four Corps areas, but was heaviest in I, II, and III Corps where the proximity of the border and the Ho Chi Minh Trail was an obvious advantage for the

enemy. Hanoi certainly did not expect a quick victory, nor had they planned for any major objective in I, II, and III Corps. But Hanoi was ready to quickly exploit any substantial gain anywhere. Thus trying to guess the Communist intention or more precisely, the Communist main objective or main effort would have been meaningless. Instead our effort had to be aimed at having a sound defense concept in all the military regions with overall centralized control and coordination. Unfortunately there was not a sound defense plan and there was no centralized control and coordination in the Joint General Staff. President Thieu was the lone controlling coordinating authority.

In all the Corps areas, the defense system was a single line of defense, not a defense in depth. All available forces were positioned in the front line, no second defensive line was planned, and no reserve force was organized at the Corps or JGS level. Also there was no evacuation plan or withdrawal and delaying action plan. Those responsible certainly did not realize that no matter how strong it may be, a rigid line of defense can hardly withstand a vigorous initial wave of attack, and that without depth to absorb this initial shock, or without contingent evacuation plans to evade and whittle down the initial shock, a single front line defensive system will generally succumb to a sustained attack.

The following account attempts to trace the collapse of this "rigid line of defense," beginning with the loss of Phuoc Long's provincial capital on January 6, 1975. In the view of several respondents, the loss of that city marked the onset of South Vietnam's disintegration.

A "sparsely populated province of about 50,000 inhabitants," Phuoc Long was located in III Corps to the north of Saigon and was considered "untenable in case of a heavy attack due to its geographical position." Its capital had been "isolated and practically encircled by enemy forces for months before its capture. Supplies to the civilian population had at times been flown in and convoys had to be organized with heavy military escort to get supplies into the province by road."[1] Phuoc Long was "weakly defended" and offered little resistance to the overwhelming Communist forces

[1] According to Buu Vien.

160

(supported by tanks and artillery) which eventually overran it.

Buu Vien considered the loss of this province capital to be of major import:

> The Communists in their move to test the will of the RVN armed forces, and especially to gauge reaction of the U.S. government, had indeed chosen an easy target. The loss of Phuoc Long was of great significance. It was the first time in the history of the Vietnam war that an entire province had been lost to the Communists and it obviously was a flagrant violation of the cease-fire agreement by the Communists. Yet the RVN armed forces command chose not to react militarily while the U.S. government due to domestic difficulties did not make any significant move to deter the Communists from further aggression.

When asked about the decision not to defend Phuoc Long, one high-ranking member of the JGS stated that the province capital had been threatened by two North Vietnamese divisions, and it was the consensus of all military commanders at the time that it could not be successfully reinforced. All the reserves were committed to I Corps and there was insufficient time to mount a successful relief, although some Airborne Rangers were eventually lifted into the town at the last moment to help with the defense.

In the view of this officer, ARVN did not possess the capability in 1975 to relieve threatened province capitals as it had done in 1973.

Expanding on the considerations that led to the decision not to defend Phuoc Long, Buu Vien reported that President Thieu had discussed the problem in a Ministers' meeting. Thieu had explained that while it was "not impossible to reoccupy" Phuoc Long, "militarily speaking, it was not worthwhile":

> At least two infantry regiments would have to be deployed in the operation and the troops would have to be dropped by air. Given the enemy forces in the area, we should expect strong reaction from the enemy and casualties would be heavy. Once the province was recaptured, troops would be needed there to defend it. This would not only immobilize a number of ARVN units, but at the same time

create serious problems of supplying the troops there. It would be better to save the troops to take care of other areas which had more strategical value.

Buu Vien stated that he for one strongly disagreed with this decision. He believed the abandonment of Phuoc Long had probably been seen by the Communists as a sign of weakness of ARVN and strongly influenced them in their decision to move forward. "At the same time," he said, "it caused our troops to lose much of their enthusiasm and their confidence in their capability" and "created a harmful psychological effect on the population":

> While urging the population to organize demonstrations all over the country demanding reoccupation of Phuoc Long, the government itself did not take any concrete action against the enemy. People began to lose confidence in what the government said and lost faith in the capability of the armed forces to protect the country. After Phuoc Long, many people became skeptical about the intent of the government, and angry people engaged in talk about Phuoc Long being sold out to the Communists.

But the action at Phuoc Long was also significant in other respects. A senior VNAF commander reported that he "lost a lot of aircraft at Phuoc Long" (some 20 planes) because of antiaircraft and SA-7 missiles. He noted that the SA-7 was almost "impossible to suppress." It was precisely this fear of antiaircraft and missile fire that forced South Vietnamese pilots to fly high and miss targets at critical points during the final offensive.

For another Vietnamese officer, Phuoc Long was a telling manifestation of the GVN's inability to carry out combined operations. As special assistant to the Inspector General of the JGS, Colonel Nguyen Huy Loi was directed to investigate the reasons why the aforementioned lift of additional Airborne Rangers into Phuoc Long by helicopter had gone so badly just before the province capital fell. His investigation revealed that "no one was responsible for this operation," and that the needed helicopters had not arrived on time or in sufficient numbers to carry the troops scheduled for the lift. Maintenance people hadn't done their job, and the various helicopter, air division, and other commanders charged with the operation were "not serious" and "didn't carry out properly their missions." In Colonel Loi's words, "the main mistake is from the Air Force and secondly from headquarters of III Corps because the III Corps is responsible for this operation. They didn't have a man to coordinate the whole operation. They didn't check out everything before the operation. So when the helicopters didn't arrive on time they worried about this and they ran around but no one [was] responsible. This is the failure." When asked to sum up the conclusions he drew from his investigation, Colonel Loi stated, "I felt this was a kind of hopeless operation and that they had tried to carry out something that the Americans did before but this time without their support. We just landed these people there and it was up to them to try to do what they could. And we knew that we cannot support them."

Chapter 9

The Loss of Ban Me Thuot

The Loss of Ban Me Thuot

While Phuoc Long was considered the most significant precursor to the 1975 offensive, all respondents agreed that the attack on Ban Me Thuot (the capital of Darlac province) on March 10 was the opening of the main event. This incident was to set into motion a chain of decisions and military moves that would have disastrous consequences for the continued resistance of South Vietnam. As one senior JGS officer put it, the attack initiated a "domino effect" which resulted in the unraveling of the country.

II Corps, where Ban Me Thuot was located, presented difficult defense problems for the GVN in that the area was large, the terrain favorable to the enemy, the provincial capitals widely separated, and the major road networks linking these strategic points vulnerable to "easy" interdiction. As a result, the security of II Corps was heavily dependent on accurate intelligence of Communist troop movements and the capability to rapidly reinforce threatened positions by airlift. Mobility was particularly important in that the Corps was comparatively lightly protected. In the words of Colonel Le Khac Ly, the II Corps Chief of Staff, there were simply "not enough forces to defend everywhere."

Only two regular ARVN divisions were stationed in II Corps, and these, along with some seven Ranger groups (each of regimental size) and one armored brigade, were required to cover widely dispersed areas. The Corps' largest division, the 22nd Infantry, which had four regiments, was committed to the defense of the heavily populated lowland provinces of Phu Yen and Binh Dinh, the latter being a traditional site of strong Communist military activity. Of the three regiments of the 23rd Infantry Division, two were deployed at Pleiku for the defense of that province and the third was stationed at Ban Me Thuot in Darlac province. The majority of the Ranger groups (usually four or five) were situated in Kontum province.

By early 1975, the Communist forces deployed in II Corps numbered five divisions (the NT3, F10, 320th, 968th, and 316th) plus an additional fifteen independent regiments consisting of armored, artillery, antiaircraft, and engineering units. Total Communist manpower in the area was estimated by Colonel Ly to be between 75,000 and 80,000 men, of which some 36,000 were in regular units. As in I and III Corps, the enemy had made major improvements in its lines of communication in the II Corps area during the period following the signing of the Paris Agreements and as a result had acquired a capability to rapidly shift armored and other strike forces between the western provinces bordering the major north-south Communist logistic routes.

Taking advantage of the improved road networks and with the help of some local Montagnard scouts,[2] the Communists had managed to position three divisions (the 320th, 316th, and F10) in Darlac province by the beginning of March. With these forces in place around Ban Me Thuot, they then commenced to cut all the major road networks in the highlands. On March 4, they established blocking positions east and west of the An Khe Pass on the road linking Pleiku to Qui Nhon (Route 19); on March 5, they severed Route 21 between Ban Me Thuot and Ninh Hoa; and on March 7, they completed their interdiction operations by blocking Route 14 between Pleiku and Ban Me Thuot.

While these road-cutting operations and other intelligence indicators had alerted II Corps to expect a major Communist offensive, there was considerable uncertainty and difference of opinion as to where the blow would fall. The II Corps Commander, Major General Phu, was convinced Pleiku would be the target, while others on his staff and in Saigon were persuaded it would be Ban

[2] This information came from Montagnard official Hantho Touneh.

168

Me Thuot or the capital of Quang Duc province further to the south. Among those believing Ban Me Thuot would be the objective were intelligence specialists on the JGS, who read the available indicators (including prisoner interrogations, captured documents, and radio intercepts) as clearly identifying this city to be the focus of Communist interest. Persuaded by this information, the JGS made several unsuccessful attempts to warn II Corps of the threat to Ban Me Thuot. However, the Chief of Staff of II Corps recollected that these JGS warnings were always qualified as "probable" and did not pinpoint Ban Me Thuot as the only target:

> I have been 21 years in the Army, and you know how the intelligence people are—"the enemy may attack such and such targets." Several places were mentioned, not only Ban Me Thuot, and Phu didn't pay any attention to such an estimate, saying, "Ah, that's too many."

Aside from being unconvinced by the intelligence specialists, General Phu was reluctant to reinforce Ban Me Thuot because this would require uncovering his defenses in Pleiku and Kontum, which were by this time under constant enemy harassment and also vulnerable to attack.[3] Since the II Corps headquarters was located in Pleiku, Phu felt "his prestige was there," and therefore he was reluctant to weaken its defenses. In the words of his Chief of Staff, Colonel Ly:

> He did not want to be a defeated general, if the enemy attacked his command post. We didn't have enough forces to defend everywhere and according to the information that we got, the enemy had about two divisions, massed west of Pleiku, around Duc Co and Plei Me, they wanted to attack posts like that. He was also afraid of the enemy's tanks because if the enemy used tanks to attack Pleiku it was ideal terrain.

---

[3] A perception the Communists attempted to encourage with feinting attacks and by leaving the main radio station of the 320th Division behind in the Pleiku area for deception purposes.

Phu also apparently believed that, on the U.S. pattern, he could rapidly reinforce Ban Me Thuot by air in the event of an attack—an assumption subsequent events were to prove quite erroneous.

Thus, despite the fact that General Phu had visited Ban Me Thuot shortly before it was attacked and had "learned about the newest information concerning the enemy concentration" around the provincial capital, he provided only minimal reinforcements to the area. One Ranger group had been moved to the town of Buon Ho down Route 14 as a precautionary measure, and one regiment of the 23rd Division (the 53rd) had been deployed to Phuong Duc airfield some five miles east of the city. An Advanced Command Post of the 23rd Division with a staff of about 300 officers and men was located within Ban Me Thuot proper, as were some three companies of Regional Forces and several platoons of Popular Forces. As the rear base of the 23rd Division, Ban Me Thuot also contained the dependents of that division, a factor that was to seriously undermine GVN attempts to relieve the town.

Following a powerful artillery barrage, Ban Me Thuot was attacked by armored and infantry units of two NVA divisions in the early morning hours of March 10. Most of the defensive positions in the town were overrun by the end of the first day. The Advanced Command Post of the 23rd Division held out until it was mistakenly bombed by VNAF aircraft attempting to provide close air support. This accidental air strike cut all the defenders' communications and completely disrupted any further organized defense. It was most unfortunate in that the troops at the Command Post were "fighting with good spirit there," and, according to Colonel Ly, the Deputy Division Commander Colonel Quang had reported by radio shortly before the strike that "we are in good shape."

In their assault on Ban Me Thuot, the Communist forces had adopted a new tactic of bypassing outer defense posts and striking immediately into the heart of the city itself. They had surrounded the 53rd Regiment at Phuong Duc airfield with strong holding forces, however, and prevented this unit from moving to the relief of Ban Me Thuot. While the 53rd "could not leave the airfield," it

170

was able to hold out for a number of days until its defenses were finally reduced.

One relief force, however, was able to get into Ban Me Thuot. The Ranger group at Buon Ho fought its way down Route 14 and was advancing into Ban Me Thuot when it was allegedly called off from the counterattack by the 23rd Division Commander, Brigadier General Tuong, who ordered it to secure a landing zone outside the town to protect the evacuation of his wife and children. This diversion nullified any future possibility of a counterattack from the Ranger unit and was the subject of much criticism from the II Corps Chief of Staff:

> . . . General Tuong, the 23rd Division Commander, worried a lot about his family. His wife and children were still in Ban Me Thuot city. So he had them go to the training center southeast of Ban Me Thuot. He had them gather there in an open place. He then directed the Ranger group to go back to the training center in order to protect the landing zone for his helicopter to pick the family up. The Ranger group was advancing, they were fighting with the enemy. The enemy was not strong inside the city. Most Communist main forces were outside the city possibly afraid to concentrate within Ban Me Thuot for fear of air attacks. Tuong directed the Rangers from the air to go back to the training center. The commander must obey the order of his general, his division commander. They went back to protect the landing zone, and he picked up his family and when the soldiers tried to go back to Ban Me Thuot city, the enemy had sealed it off.

Meanwhile, prodded by President Thieu to reoccupy Ban Me Thuot, General Phu began to airlift elements of the 23rd Division's 44th Regiment from Pleiku into Phuoc An, a town about 20 miles east of Ban Me Thuot on Route 21. Apparently, General Phu planned to lift the entire regiment to Phuoc An within three days and from there link up with the 53rd Regiment, which was still holding out at the airfield east of Ban Me Thuot. However, this relief operation was said to have been badly conceived and could not be executed. Helicopter assets were limited, so less than two battalions could be carried to Phuoc An in the allotted time, and these could be provided with no artillery or tank support. Commenting on this operation, the II Corps Chief of Staff stated:

> . . .[General Phu] did not foresee that it might take longer to accomplish this and we would need reinforcements and logistical support for the troops. And no way with the roads cut, we could not get supplies from Nha Trang to that regiment. And even if we wanted to reinforce it, no way. The air assets were very limited, and kept dropping every day. The first day we had seven or eight Chinooks, the next day it dropped to five, next day to three, then two and one. Because of mechanical problems, and that was a big mistake.

But even more disastrous, the troops lifted into Phuoc An "were not ready to fight" and began to desert in order to take care of their families. As another officer, General Thinh, described the situation:

> Ban Me Thuot was the rear base of the 23rd Division, with many barracks of married men from all the units. For this reason, it was hoped that the men would push quickly toward the city in order to liberate their families in the city. Unfortunately, the opposite took place. As soon as they landed with their copters, . . . most of the soldiers, seeing by chance their families who had left the city several days earlier, threw their uniforms and weapons away and disguised themselves as civilians in order to lead their wives and children to Nha Trang, which city was still under friendly control.

The Chief of Staff of II Corps confirmed this breakdown in discipline:

> . . . the defensive troops worried too much about their families in Ban Me Thuot city. So when they got out of the helicopters they would run to find their wives and children rather than fighting the enemy. When they departed from Pleiku the spirit of fighting was very high, the morale was very high. And Tuong and Phu felt very good about it. But actually, when they got on the ground at Ban Me

172

Thuot, they ran away to take care of their families. Nobody could control them.

Desertions out of concern for the welfare of dependents, first manifested in Phuoc An, became a frequent story in the weeks following the attack and were a critical factor in the erosion of ARVN defensive capabilities in other areas of the country.

While General Phu undoubtedly did not expect his forces to desert, he nevertheless seems to have harbored reservations about the overall operation to relieve Ban Me Thuot. In a conversation with a II Corps colleague, who was also a general officer, on March 12, when the airlift was in process, Phu indicated that the only reason he was sending troops to Phuoc An was because President Thieu had ordered him to reoccupy Ban Me Thuot. Phu stated that he was operating under a major disadvantage in that he had "no information" on the size of the enemy forces in the area and was pessimistic about the chances of reoccupying the province capital. Besides, even at this late date, General Phu said he still believed that the attack on Ban Me Thuot was a diversionary effort and the main target of the enemy was Pleiku.

As would be expected in any discussion of an operation that had gone wrong in so many respects, many respondents were critical of the manner in which the defense and relief of Ban Me Thuot had been managed. Several believed that General Phu committed a serious blunder in not reinforcing Ban Me Thuot before it was attacked, and they felt that his relief operation into Phuoc An was "very badly conducted" and planned. They considered the insertion of forces into Phuoc An, west of the Communist blocking positions on Route 21, to have been a major tactical error in that it denied these units necessary artillery and armor support.[4] Instead, the respondents felt, it would have been far better to have attempted to reopen Route 21 with a combined armored task force moving up from Nha Trang.

One respondent, Colonel Loi of the JGS, attributed Phu's tacti-

---

[4] As one officer put it, "All this infantry without artillery or tank support was just wandering around Phuoc An and could do nothing."

cal errors to the mistaken belief that II Corps could still mount a fast-reaction airlift operation "without American support":

> That is a very important point. The Vietnamese commanders did not realize that they could not operate in the same way. They still thought they could operate like the Americans.

Even the mildest critics felt that General Phu acted "without adequate information," and one faulted the lack of coordination between air and ground units due to inadequate communications. Close air support to Ban Me Thuot, which had numbered 200 sorties on March 10, dropped to only 60 or 70 sorties on the following days, because "of lack of information about the enemy position as well as the movement of the fighting to populated areas which considerably constrained the air intervention."[5]

The performance of the 23rd Division Commander, General Tuong, was also the subject of severe censure by several respondents, not only because he had diverted the Rangers from their counterattack in Ban Me Thuot, but also because Tuong himself had left the battlefield at Phuoc An after receiving a slight facial wound. In the words of General Thinh, he "had himself sent to a hospital after his helicopter was touched by an enemy machine gun bullet. He received only a slight surface wound which required only a simple dressing, not hospitalization. But this permitted him to avoid responsibility for [the] certain defeat of his division."

---

[5] As reported by Colonel Uoc.

Chapter 10

Thieu's Decision to Redeploy

Thieu's Decision to Redeploy

The attack on Ban Me Thuot was the catalyst for a fundamental change in President Thieu's strategy for the defense of South Vietnam. It led him to abandon the policy of "no territorial concession" embodied in his dictum of the "Four No's" and to order a major redeployment of GVN forces in both II and I Corps. While Ban Me Thuot triggered this change in strategy, there is evidence that Thieu was contemplating adjustments in his defensive positions at least a month earlier. A senior general reported that prior to the Tet holiday in February, Thieu had mentioned to him the need for a "new strategy" to "concentrate regular forces and abandon isolated areas" because the Communists had moved "a lot of divisions into the South." Thieu provided no details as to his specific plans but did ask the general's opinion about the possibility of "giving up Kontum." He told the general he would meet with him and "some other generals to make plans" about redeployments after Tet. Nothing came of this, however, and Thieu did not contact him prior to the attack on Ban Me Thuot.

Concern about the NVA buildup and, in particular, about the mounting Communist pressure in the Tay Ninh area of III Corps, however, did, according to some respondents, prompt Thieu and the JGS to decide in early March to return the Airborne Division from I Corps to Saigon. Although it had been stationed in I Corps since the Easter offensive of 1972, the Airborne was still considered to be the JGS's primary contingency force, and I Corps had previously been warned to be prepared to release this reserve force upon 72 hours notice. On March 10, I Corps received orders to return the Airborne to Saigon. This redeployment was to be completed within a period of less than two weeks.

Commenting on the circumstances leading to this decision, Buu Vien stated:

> Along with the attack of Phuoc Long, fighting became more and more intense around Tay Ninh province. Unlike Phuoc Long, Tay Ninh was considered as a strategically important province that had to be defended at all costs. Its loss would directly threaten the security of the Capital Military District.
>
> Even though the enemy had already succeeded in occupying several key positions around the provincial capital, especially the Black Virgin mountain which overlooked the city and where ARVN had its radar installation, he still wasn't able to get through to the city, thanks to the valiant resistance of the defending units, particularly those of the 25th ARVN division under the command of General Ly Tong Ba. Ba was one of the most able ARVN generals. It was he who had successfully defended Kontum with the 23rd ARVN division under his command, had driven off the Communists from the city in the 1972 Communist offensive.
>
> But the pressure exerted by the enemy with heavy artillery shelling into the city created a population exodus to Binh Duong and Saigon and shook the morale of the Cao Dai dignitaries who were quick to declare the site of the Cao Dai Temple neutral to military activities.
>
> As enemy pressure persisted, President Thieu deemed it necessary to strengthen the defense of the capital area and decided to pull the Airborne Division back from MR I to Saigon.

While other respondents agreed with Buu Vien's view that the withdrawal was motivated by military necessity, several senior officers were equally convinced that Thieu's primary consideration in calling for the return of the reserves was to guard against the possibility of a coup. Whatever the motivation, the recall of the Airborne had a profound effect on subsequent events in I Corps and contributed importantly to "unhinging" the defense of that area.

Even though Thieu seemed to have been contemplating other

shifts in GVN defensive dispositions, it was the attack on Ban Me Thuot that precipitated him to action. In the words of one high-ranking general, "the fate of South Vietnam" was determined by a decision made at a meeting at the Presidential Palace on the morning of March 11. At this meeting, which was attended by JGS Chairman General Cao Van Vien, Lieutenant General Dang Van Quang, and Prime Minister Khiem, the President is reported to have put a map on the table and told those in attendance that he considered Ban Me Thuot more important than Pleiku and that II Corps (i.e., General Phu) must retake it "at all cost." He went on to state that III and IV Corps were very important to South Vietnam's future (and must be defended) because of the offshore oil deposits and because they comprised the country's rice bowl. President Thieu then pointed to the more important coastal areas of I Corps, which he said should also be held. Thus the President had come to the view that South Vietnam could no longer protect all its territory and some redeployment of forces to defend the most important areas was now necessary.

When asked to speculate on why the President had finally come to this conclusion, one senior staff officer replied that he thought it was because Thieu no longer had hope for American aid. Previously, on the basis of the assurances he had received from President Nixon, Thieu had thought the United States would react to a Communist attack,[6] but after a recent visit from a U.S. Congressional delegation, he knew this was no longer in the cards.

That Thieu's decision stemmed from concern about the adverse balance of forces prevailing in the country and from a pessimistic reading of the likelihood of further U.S. assistance was also confirmed by Nguyen Ba Can. As Speaker of the House of Representatives and a Presidium member of the ruling party, Can had frequent meetings with Thieu and claims he was "one of the few to whom President Thieu confided his deeper thoughts on political matters." Thieu consulted Can the day after the Palace meeting (March 12) in order to discuss the "rapidly deteriorating situation" in the country and, as Can only later realized, in order to get

[6] A letter containing such assurances from President Nixon had been circulated to key officials in the South Vietnamese government.

179

"the House's concurrence in the historic decision he intended to take two days later" at Cam Ranh Bay when he ordered the redeployment from Pleiku and Kontum.

In Can's view, Thieu's decision to redeploy his forces "cannot be regarded as an inspiration of the moment, nor as a move by an exhausted man stunned by the loss of Ban Me Thuot. Rather it must be viewed as the result of his revised strategic assessment of the general situation of the country and mainly of the balance of forces that had become severely tipped in favor of North Vietnam." Moreover, there was a "disastrous morale crisis prevailing in South Vietnam at that time as a result of the aid reductions." In their frequent meetings, Thieu told Speaker Can "that only a consistent U.S. support effort would deter North Vietnam from launching an all-out offensive."

But in addition to these military imperatives, Can asserted that there "must have been highly important political necessities that motivated Thieu's decision to retreat":

> At the time, Thieu was in a very bad posture. The growing opposition was about to urge him to resign. Moreover, word of a coup spread around Saigon, and additional U.S. aid seemed to be uncertain despite tremendous efforts by President Ford to convince the Congress that more aid was vitally needed.
>
> Besides satisfying the purely military needs, Thieu's decision to abandon the highlands . . . would also aim at creating a state of emergency in the country which would consequently muzzle the mounting opposition. What was more, Thieu would expect that because of worldwide repercussions resulting from the catastrophic retreat, the U.S. would appropriate the requested military aid in order to avoid being accused of betraying an ally and thus losing all confidence abroad.
>
> Since Phuoc Long had fallen into enemy hands, President Thieu . . . repeatedly blamed his reverses on Washington's failure to keep its promises, and once exploded: "If they [the U.S.] grant full aid we will hold the whole country, but if they only give half of it, we will only hold half the country." [Can was] surprised by such reasoning which sounded as though President Thieu was defending the U.S. and was fighting for the Americans themselves.

A few other respondents also believed that one of the key motivating factors in the redeployment of forces, particularly with respect to Pleiku and Kontum, was Thieu's desire to generate a climate of crisis and impel the United States to supply more aid—in the words of one general officer, "a ploy for the ideas of the U.S. Congress." But most of the respondents doubted that this was a major consideration and saw Thieu's decision as an attempt to tighten his defense lines. Buu Vien, for example, thought Thieu wanted "to give up land to save troops," and Colonel Nhan stated, "Thieu obviously believed that the retreat simply meant to preserve the fighting forces in order to defend a smaller area of land more effectively." Indeed, President Thieu had demonstrated a propensity toward such tactics during an earlier period of the war. The general officer who was III Corps Commander during the 1972 offensive revealed that Thieu had ordered him "three times" to withdraw his forces from embattled An Loc in order to "save" them for the defense of Saigon. Believing such a retreat would be disastrous for troop morale and discipline, this commander had been able to resist this order only by threatening his resignation.

Following the Palace meeting on March 11, Thieu moved rapidly during the next few days to order major redeployments in both I and II Corps. On March 13, he called the I Corps Commander, Lieutenant General Truong, back to Saigon and informed him that "he had to give up most of I Corps." The President's order was apparently explicit—I Corps was to keep only Danang, its seaport, and the immediate surrounding area. President Thieu had decided, according to the I corps Chief of Staff, that

> . . . the new strategy was to "lighten the top." The idea of that strategy was to "keep the bottom." This term was used by President Thieu, for the country, that meant that Saigon was the bottom. And in I Corps, it meant that the bottom piece was Danang. . . . So what Saigon was for the whole country, Danang was for I Corps.

Truong was instructed to develop a plan for executing the necessary redeployments to defend Danang immediately upon

181

return to his headquarters. While he apparently did not protest at the time, General Truong reported that he was "disturbed" by this order in that he was already aware of problems resulting from the movement of refugees and dependents in the I Corps area. He knew that the situation might become even more difficult, based on the experience in the northern Corps areas during the Easter offensive of 1972.

Having set in motion the planning for redeployments in I Corps, Thieu next turned his attention to II Corps. On March 14, he met with the II Corps Commander, Major General Phu, at Cam Ranh Bay. Present at the meeting also were Lieutenant General Quang, General Vien, and Prime Minister Khiem. No staff officers were allowed to attend, as General Phu had received strict orders that the President wanted to meet with him "alone."

While some elements of the Cam Ranh meeting were disputed by various respondents, it seems clear that the following basic decisions were made there: (1) The regular forces (the remaining elements of the 23rd Division, the Rangers, and the Armor Brigade) were to be withdrawn from Pleiku and Kontum and moved to the coast, with the aim of eventually retaking Ban Me Thuot; (2) the Regional and Popular Forces, along with dependents, civilians, and elements of the GVN administrative structure in Pleiku and Kontum, were not to be withdrawn; (3) the redeployment was to be implemented secretly and conducted within a few days in order to "surprise the enemy"; and (4) the route of the redeployment would be Route 7B, a long-unused road leading from Pleiku to Tuy Hoa. The selection of this road was also to "gain surprise."

The major issue in dispute concerning the Cam Ranh meeting was whether Thieu ordered General Phu to abandon Pleiku and Kontum or just to redeploy forces to retake Ban Me Thuot. According to one version, Thieu gave his Corps commander orders to "reoccupy Ban Me Thuot at all costs" but did not order Phu to withdraw from Pleiku and Kontum, per se. But other respondents, including the investigating officer who read General Phu's declaration concerning the Cam Ranh meeting, recalled Phu claiming that withdrawal was indeed intended.[7] However, Phu's account of Cam Ranh seems self-serving and was not corroborated by his Chief of Staff, Colonel Ly, who recalled General Phu asserting that the President's order was to redeploy forces to Nha Trang so that they could plan to retake Ban Me Thuot. Whatever the exact order, the issue is somewhat academic in that all participants must have realized that any major redeployment of additional forces from Pleiku and Kontum would necessarily result in the eventual loss of those two towns. Indeed, Thieu acknowledged this to be the import of his decision in his farewell address on April 21, 1975:

> After Ban Me Thuot fell we wondered where we could get troops to recapture it. We came to a political decision not to insure the life or death defense of Kontum or Pleiku. . . . We decided to redeploy our forces from Kontum and Pleiku to recapture Ban Me Thuot. If Ban Me Thuot were retaken, we believed, we would have the opportunity to retake Kontum and Pleiku.[8]

Moreover, the fact that Pleiku and Kontum were not to be "abandoned" and all forces were not to withdraw was explained by the apparently agreed-upon strategy that the Regional and Popular Forces, who were Montagnard, were to be left behind to screen the withdrawal.

One of the most severely criticized aspects of the Cam Ranh decision was the selection of Route 7B as the withdrawal route. This road had long been abandoned, and was in a general state of disrepair; it had been mined by forces on both sides and was in need of extensive bridge work. According to one high-ranking officer, the initial suggestion for using Route 7B came from

[7] Colonel Loi, who was the investigating officer, reported that in his brief declaration to the JGS, Phu claimed he told Thieu at Cam Ranh, "We can hold out and we can defend Pleiku." However, the President rejected this course of action, responding, "Now the American aid is cut off and now we have lost Ban Me Thuot we have to retreat to reduce the front. And we have to get out of Pleiku. So try to bring all your forces down to the coast."

[8] FBIS, Asia and Pacific, APA-75-78, April 22, 1975, p. 19.

General Phu, who favored this route because the enemy was "not there" and it provided "the advantage of surprise."[9] General Phu told a II Corps colleague (on March 16) that Route 7B had been selected both for surprise and because President Thieu had ordered the redeployment to be accomplished within a couple of days. Phu told this officer, "I didn't have a choice—the President said I had only two days in which to accomplish the withdrawal." Alternative redeployment routes had been discussed at the Cam Ranh meeting, but none were acceptable to Phu. In fact, however, none of those in attendance at Cam Ranh seem to have protested the selection of Route 7B, and it was reported that both General Vien and President Thieu agreed with Phu's decision to use that road. But at least one participant at the Cam Ranh meeting seems to have harbored some reservations about the operation's chance of success. According to a general officer who discussed the Cam Ranh meeting with General Phu several days after the event, General Phu had been told that "if he succeeded in withdrawing only 50 percent of the military personnel and vehicles he would be a hero." When told this by the II Corps Commander, this officer responded to Phu that he would "not be a hero" but would "lose your command by this withdrawal."

---

[9] This account appears to be confirmed by General Phu's later statement to his Chief of Staff that surprise would be achieved on 7B because "the enemy didn't pay attention to Phu Bon [as] this area was forgotten by the enemy and friendly, too."

Chapter 11

The Withdrawal from Pleiku and Kontum

The Withdrawal from Pleiku and Kontum

Following the meeting in Cam Ranh, General Phu flew back to his headquarters at Pleiku and at 6:00 P.M. called a meeting of his key staff officers; included were Brigadier General Cam (the Assistant for Operations), Brigadier General Sang (Commander of the 6th Air Division), Brigadier General Tat (the Ranger commander and Phu's "favorite"), and Colonel Ly, his Chief of Staff—"five people only." Phu told them the President's decision, that is, that "we would leave Pleiku and Kontum and move to Nha Trang and set up our II Corps headquarters there. Then we will plan to retake Ban Me Thuot from there."[10] With the exception of General Tat, who had met privately with General Phu upon his arrival, all of those assembled were surprised by this announcement. In the words of Colonel Ly:

> Nobody believed him. All of us asked him again, we are to abandon Kontum and Pleiku? Yes, this decision has already been made. We have no discussion on this. I asked him how? He said some by air, some by road. I asked him what road? He said Route 7B, through Phu Bon. "That has been already decided." No discussion again. It was the President's decision.

Colonel Ly, who as Chief of Staff had responsibility for planning, then said to Phu:

[10] Interview with Colonel Ly.

187

Please give me a week or three days at least for me to present you with a plan. [Phu responded,] "No. You have no time. Everything starts tomorrow." I opened my eyes widely, my mouth, and everyone looked at him, except Tat. He said, "Tomorrow I will fly to Nha Trang and Cam and Ly will stay here. Tat will be overall commander. That's the plan."

General Phu then expanded on the command arrangements for the redeployment. General Tat, who had been promoted to brigadier general at Phu's request during the Cam Ranh meeting, was given overall command of the operation. However, matters were immediately confused when Phu also gave General Cam "verbal orders to the effect that he was to 'supervise' the retreat." This, according to Colonel Ly, "created more problems between Tat and Cam, more disagreements." Phu directed his staff to "go ahead and prepare tonight and start moving tomorrow." Orders were to be issued just one hour in advance to each unit commander.

General Phu then revealed the news that only the regular units were to be withdrawn. Colonel Ly remembered this part of the conversation vividly:

I asked him another question, how about the province and district personnel, the RF/PF, the troops' dependents and the people? He said, [and] I will never forget, "Forget about them. You have no responsibility to take care of them! . . . If you tell them about it, you can't control it and you cannot get down to Tuy Hoa because there would be panic."

That evening Colonel Ly tried to dissuade General Phu from using Route 7B; he urged Phu instead to attempt the withdrawal along Route 19, which he believed could be opened by simultaneous clearing operations from Pleiku in the west and from the 22nd Division in the east. He argued that Route 19 was a better road, whereas Route 7B

. . . required a lot of engineer effort to open the road, because [of] mines, enemy mines, friendly mines, and Special Force mines. The bridges were also down and the route had not been used for a

188

long time. So we had to rebuild it. And it would take time and equipment to rebuild. Engineering equipment. Do we have enough, can we move it? If the American troops were here, they could use flying cranes for the movement of engineer equipment into the area. It would be easy. But now, we the Vietnamese are alone, do we have enough assets to move heavy equipment to the place where it is needed? That's a problem. It's good for surprise, I agree with you. Yes, surprise. For the enemy to move into this area to attack us would take time. But we have to build roads, to build bridges, and it's easy for them to harass us. The enemy will have enough time to overcome the surprise. But he didn't buy my opinions. He said the President had already decided.

When asked if II Corps had sufficient engineers and equipment to repair Route 7B, Colonel Ly responded:

We did not have enough. We had just a fair amount of equipment and engineers. It requires a lot of time, it's a tough job. To move equipment it takes time. It's heavy equipment and can't move fast. He [Phu] said the President discussed that, knew that. The President and Vien knew that, they all knew about the difficulties and they decided to take this road, a big surprise to the enemy. We would be down to Tuy Hoa by the time the enemy came and we would have no problem at all. We would use air support.

The next morning, at about 7:00, General Phu flew to Nha Trang, taking with him a number of key staff officers. Angered at Phu's command arrangements, General Cam (the overall "supervisor") also decided to depart and flew to Tuy Hoa, telling the Chief of Staff, "Ly, you take care of everything. I will see you there. I am just a supervisor." At this point, Colonel Ly saw himself burdened with almost the entire responsibility for the withdrawal—with no staff, no planning, and no guidance from the JGS staff in Saigon, who themselves were at first unaware of Thieu's redeployment order. As the II Corps Chief of Staff described the situation:

. . . Tat, he got his star, and he got to take care of his Rangers. And I was the only man to assume the responsibility for everything

189

else. Cam to Tuy Hoa, Phu to Nha Trang, and Tat stayed at the old American 4th Division headquarters in Pleiku (Ham Rong mountain) to take care of his Rangers. I stayed of course in Corps headquarters. Every report from all units came to me and they reported, "Enemy attack, enemy attack—surrounded." I could communicate with General Phu on the "hot line" phone only. And Saigon said they could not get information from Phu in Nha Trang. I forgot to tell you one more thing. Phu took with him all the key staff members. The Chiefs of G3, G2, G1, all his key staff went with him. He left only the deputies of each staff agency with me. The total troops we had in II Corps at that time was about 165,000 including lowland troops. And you withdraw a Corps like that with no planning! With no planning at all he withdrew the troops. I had to do my best. I called the unit commanders, I had to let them know the situation. I personally informed the Americans there, the CIA, the consulate, the DAO, and told them they must go right now. At first they couldn't believe me. But I said, "Go, don't ask." They called Saigon and checked with headquarters, and they didn't know. . . . Later on of course, they knew and they were asking me questions, "Where is Phu?," and I said, "Phu is *not* here, Phu is in Nha Trang." And Phu couldn't provide enough information for the JGS. So the JGS contacted me directly in Pleiku.

Once Colonel Ly informed the unit commanders that they had to prepare to move, panic broke out in Pleiku. Realizing that they were to be abandoned, the Montagnard Regional and Popular Forces began to riot. In Colonel Ly's words, "the people, the troops, the dependents became undisciplined. Troops were raping, burning things and committing robbery. The troops became undisciplined when they heard the order. I can't blame them. There was no plan to take care of the troops' dependents." Disorder also quickly spread to the Pleiku airfield where Colonel Ly was attempting to evacuate equipment and personnel by C-130 aircraft flown from Saigon. According to Colonel Ly:

> The airfield at Pleiku was in a state of panic. Sometimes the planes could land, but they couldn't do the job. I had to go there and use my pistol to restore order. Of course, I didn't shoot anybody, just shot in the air. And when the people saw me, there was order. But

190

soon I had to go back to headquarters. And the enemy kept shelling the headquarters at Pleiku and the airfield. That was the reason we could not move everything we wanted out from Pleiku. We left all the old airplanes in Pleiku, helicopters and fixed wing, and heavy equipment, and the important equipment like the sensors left by the Special Forces. All types of equipment like that. We moved only about 70 percent of what we had. What we left behind we destroyed by air later.[11]

After first dispatching engineer units down Route 7B to repair the disabled bridges, Colonel Ly began the withdrawal from Pleiku and Kontum on March 16. The movement of forces was scheduled over a three-day period (March 16 to 18), and various combat, logistic, and staff components were assigned specific departure dates. Most of the Rangers were positioned toward the end of the column. However, Colonel Ly had no time to properly plan the operation and received little help from General Tat:

General Phu didn't know anything about it. He believed Tat would take care of everything. But Tat didn't do anything. Tat told me—Tat and I were classmates—Tat said, "You take care of it." And he took care of his own troops. There was no time to think of anything, just reaction.

The road-opening operations went slowly and the withdrawal column was soon blocked near Cheo Reo, the small provincial capital of Phu Bon province located halfway down Route 7B. Repair work on the bridges took much longer than had been anticipated:

We had a problem with the equipment. The technique to build the bridge took time. General Phu's estimate was that in about two days the roads would be open. He was completely wrong. Just one bridge took about three or four days.

[11] However, Colonel Uoc reported that not all "operational planes" were destroyed at Pleiku and that "over 100,000 tons of ammunition" were left behind.

191

In the meantime, a mass of refugees from Kontum and Pleiku had begun to join the movement down 7B. To quote Ly, "Before noontime on the first day [March 16] the road started to have people moving on [it]. And by that night and the next day many, many people—troop dependents, people, all kinds of transportation, even baby carriages were on the road. And every day from that day on."

Recovering from their initial surprise at II Corps' decision to retreat down Route 7B (which they had previously considered to be unusable), the Communists rapidly deployed elements of the NVA 320th Division to attack Cheo Reo on March 17 and harass the withdrawal column. Jammed with civilians and military alike, the road from Pleiku rapidly became a nightmare. Unit integrity completely disintegrated as did all semblance of control. "There was no way to keep a well-organized column." Recalling the scene, Colonel Ly stated:

> The road from Pleiku was terrible. I saw many old people and babies fall down on the road and tanks and trucks would go over them. Accidents all the time but everything would keep moving. . . . Nobody could control anything. No order. The troops were mixed with the dependents and civilians and were trying to take care of all the children and wives. You can't imagine it. It was terrible. No control. And the enemy squeezed them. Refugees were strung out all the way from Cheo Reo back to the point where 7B and Route 14 fork. I walked under fire.

The Ranger units bringing up the rear of the column attempted to bypass the mass of civilians on the road to help with the growing Communist pressure on Cheo Reo, but the units were "blocked by the many people" and "couldn't move." Food supplies for the retreating forces were insufficient, and after two days "most of the soldiers were starving and had to pillage the highlander villages along Route 7."[12] Instances of violence and rape were also common.

An armored unit fighting to open the road east of Cheo Reo

[12] As reported by General Thinh.

became disorganized when it was mistakenly hit by VNAF pilots "flying too high." Four tanks were destroyed and a number of troops and civilians killed. This act, in Colonel Ly's words, "made morale very, very bad."

By the time Colonel Ly arrived in Cheo Reo on March 18, he found a "mass of population" crammed into the immediate area. "About 200,000 people around at one small place." The situation was chaotic: Some troops were looting, and the Communists were shelling the town. On the evening of March 19, with Communist forces within a half mile of the town, General Phu ordered the evacuation of Colonel Ly and other senior officers from Cheo Reo by helicopter.

In the ensuing days, the retreating military units and civilians continued to stagger down Route 7B toward Tuy Hoa. The necessary bridges were eventually repaired, so that some could escape, but most were killed or captured. The Commander of the ARVN Artillery Command, General Thinh, described the retreat as follows:

> We must salute the battalion commanders and lower officers for having marched with their units but they were no longer able to control their famished and tired men. The soldiers kept shouting insults at Thieu for this impossible and terrible retreat. Some reached the limit of their despair and killed the officers. An artillery battalion commander who was marching in the retreating column was shot to death by some Rangers who wanted his beautiful wristwatch.
>
> The despair was so great that at one point two or three guerrillas arriving at the scene could make prisoners of a hundred Rangers. Wives and children of retreating soldiers died of hunger and sickness on the road. It was a true hell.

By Colonel Ly's estimate, only about 20,000 of the 60,000 troops that had started out from Pleiku and Kontum finally got down to Tuy Hoa, and these were no longer fit for combat. Only about 700 of the estimated 7,000 Rangers escaped, along with a handful of armored vehicles, "about 30, including the APCs." Of the some 400,000 civilians who had attempted to flee Kontum,

193

Pleiku, and Phu Bon, only an estimated 100,000 got through. Whereas General Phu had calculated that the withdrawal could be accomplished within a period of "three days," military stragglers were still trickling down Route 7B when the Communists captured Tuy Hoa on April 1.

One former general officer characterized the withdrawal from Pleiku and Kontum as the "greatest disaster in the history of ARVN." Another went even further, stating it "must rank as one of the worst planned and the worst executed withdrawal operations in the annals of military history." Of all the events contributing to the collapse of Vietnam, this was the one most criticized by the respondents.

Not surprisingly, the heaviest criticism was directed at General Phu. While several respondents stated that Phu had been a "good division commander," many considered him "unfit" for a Corps command. His critics portrayed him as a man of "poor intellectual and professional capability," lacking the character or training to cope with the "grave situation" facing him in II Corps. His Chief of Staff described him as "the type of person who acts according to his sentiment rather than his logic," and "in the battlefield . . . terrible." Most of them condemned the fact that Phu was the first to flee Pleiku and did not remain with his troops to personally command the withdrawal—behavior which one respondent attributed to Phu's great fear of recapture by the Communists (he had been taken prisoner at the battle of Dien Bien Phu).[13]

There were also those who felt that the withdrawal operation should never have been left in Phu's hands in the first place, that the JGS should have played the major role. As General Don put it:

> The problem was that an operation like this should have been conducted by the General Staff with their whole support . . . that was the mistake on our side. There was no cooperation between the General Staff and the Corps headquarters.

[13] As far as Phu's personal fate is concerned, the respondents reported that he had died in the last days of the war, in Saigon—according to some, by his own hand. They also stated that he had been a very sick man, afflicted with tuberculosis, and not suited for a Corps command for health reasons, as well as for reasons of professional competence.

But the respondents also saw a more fundamental error—the decision to withdraw at all. They held that Thieu (along with the others at Cam Ranh) blundered in thinking that II Corps could withdraw forces already under enemy pressure and preserve their morale and combat effectiveness, much less retake Ban Me Thuot. General Don, for one, characterized the Cam Ranh decision as "stupid":

> We come back to the same problem. Thieu has given too much power to the Corps commanders. And the Corps commanders decided what to do and when. It is the common duty for Thieu, Vien, the Corps commanders, to study also and not let only Thieu himself to decide. It is stupid to say you will retake Ban Me Thuot and then you abandon Pleiku. You didn't retake Ban Me Thuot, you lost Pleiku.

These critics believed it would have been wiser to have remained in Pleiku and Kontum and fought. One general officer on the JGS, for example, thought this would have been by far the best alternative. He estimated that General Phu had from 15 to 30 days of supplies on hand and that some air resupply would have permitted II Corps to hold out even longer.[14] He believed that had a strong defense been mounted, this might have changed U.S. Congressional opinion and brought in more American support. Colonel Ly concurred in this view and stated that Pleiku could have held against a two-division Communist attack for "at least from two weeks to two months," even if it could not be resupplied. He felt it would have been "very costly to the Communists" to take Pleiku and that "it would have been a far better decision to stay there." Several of his subordinate officers apparently agreed with him:

> At least three or four unit commanders came to me when Phu had left Pleiku. They came to me and said, "Why do we leave?" I can't give you an answer. That's the order from high headquarters. We

[14] The JGS had calculated that Pleiku and Kontum would require 300 tons of supplies daily in sustained combat but that air resupply could provide only 100 to 150 tons a day.

have to leave. And they said, "Why, we want to fight. Even me, I want to die here. We still have enough supplies and assets to fight. The enemy cannot take over Kontum and Pleiku." I said, "What can we do?"

Chapter 12

The Subsequent Collapse of II Corps

The Subsequent Collapse of II Corps

Following the disastrous withdrawal from Pleiku and Kontum, Communist main force divisions started exerting heavy pressure on the three regiments of the ARVN 22nd Division guarding Binh Dinh province in northern II Corps.[15] (The other regiment of the 22nd Division had been redeployed to the south to assist with the defense of the Nha Trang area.) Initially, the enemy pressure came from the highlands down to the lowlands, but the 22nd Division soon also had to contend with NVA forces driving down from southern I Corps where they had been freed by the collapse of resistance in Quang Ngai. By all accounts, the officers and men of the 22nd Division "fought very well," even "valiantly," in their attempt to hold off the attacking NVA divisions.

However, strong enemy pressure, lack of supplies, and the "disorder" created by Communist sapper attacks in the Division's rear area at Qui Nhon forced the 22nd to withdraw to Qui Nhon at the end of March and attempt an evacuation by sea. In the words of General Thinh, "finally isolated, at the end of [its] supplies, and deprived of the necessary area support, it was forced to lead a heroic delaying action toward the ocean, abandoning the province of Binh Dinh to the enemy."[16] Only about 2,000 officers and men

---

[15] According to the II Corps Chief of Staff, the 22nd Division Commander, General Niem, "had one regiment in the north, north of Phu My, one regiment in Binh Khe (on Route 19), and one at Qui Nhon."

[16] In the course of this retreat, one regiment reportedly suffered heavy losses from a Communist ambush when it withdrew into Phu Cat airfield. The regiment assumed the airfield to be in friendly hands, but the air commander at Phu Cat had received a "secret order" to evacuate the base, and it had been occupied by the Communists by the time the regiment arrived.

("a fifth of its complement") could be evacuated by ship at Qui Nhon on April 1, the remaining forces having dispersed or been "killed, wounded, or made prisoner. . . . The general commanding the 22nd Division, in his command post on [the] boat, fainted several times at the news of [the] severe losses of his unit."

The situation in the central and southern areas of II Corps also began to disintegrate. According to a senior general who was stationed in II Corps at the time:

> With the loss of Ban Me Thuot, Quang Duc province in the southwest became completely isolated and immediately threatened. The situation there was untenable and Quang Duc could not possibly hold. The fall of Ban Me Thuot and Quang Duc opened the whole southern flank of II Corps area. Tuyen Duc and Lam Dong provinces were under Communist pressure. Heavy enemy infiltration with tanks, infantry, artillery, and rockets was reported in these two provinces. The Communists also were beginning to shell the two cities with rockets.

The Ranger group defending Quang Duc province "dispersed"; Lam Dong province was occupied soon thereafter, and Dalat (in Tuyen Duc province) was threatened with encirclement and eventually evacuated. However, several respondents reported that Communist forces did not actually occupy Dalat until several days after its evacuation. The Regional and Popular Forces defending these latter provinces proved no match for the Communist main force units in the area.

The South Vietnamese attempted to slow the Communist advance by air strikes on the roads and bridges leading to the coastal areas. Air operations, however, were hampered by intense enemy antiaircraft fire which was "very effective, usually up to 15,000 to 20,000 feet" and hit "most of the aircraft." Air support was also degraded by the confusion and congestion caused by the redeployment of the 6th Air Division from Pleiku to the remaining southern bases at Nha Trang and Phan Rang. Colonel Uoc portrayed this situation as follows:

> The combat forces of the two air divisions in the second military region declined from day-to-day because of the congestion caused

by too many planes, personnel, and their families. There was a shortage of mechanics and pilots because they were busy taking care of their families at Nha Trang and Phan Rang bases. As a result, there was no one to work on damaged planes, parts were lacking and pilots from a certain squadron could not fly planes of another squadron because headquarters had not yet made the arrangements. Also, because of lack of coordination some pilots and mechanics had nothing to do. In brief, that strategic withdrawal was carried out without previous organization or leadership. I, as Commander of the Air Operations Command, had presented these difficulties to the Air Force headquarters without any result because we [the Air Operations Command] needed only planes, bombs, and ammunition in order to fight. It was very sad and heartbreaking to see the Communist attack without the ability to counter. The withdrawal of the 6th Air Division to Nha Trang and Phan Rang from all aspects—morale, materiel, as well as strategic—was a complete failure.

The shortcomings in command and control mentioned above were a frequent source of complaint by the II Corps respondents. Several mentioned an absence of "clear orders" from headquarters in Saigon, which they even had difficulty contacting, and several suggested that at times "no one was in charge" of the defense.

The Communist F-10 Division, which had participated in the capture of Ban Me Thuot, began moving down Route 21 toward the coastal town of Nha Trang, the new site of the II Corps headquarters. In order to check this drive, on March 17 the JGS diverted one of the Airborne brigades being withdrawn from I Corps to Nha Trang and inserted it at a pass (near Khanh Duong) some 30 miles west of Ninh Hoa on Route 21. With a force of about 2,000 men, the brigade was soon engaged in "violent fighting" and defended its position at the pass tenaciously, knocking out many enemy tanks in the process.[17] As General Thinh described the battle:

Quite a number of T-54 tanks were hit and burned, artillery duels terminated in silence by North Vietnamese artillery but also by the

[17] All Airborne units seemed to have fought consistently well throughout the last months of the war.

losses of South Vietnamese artillery. The paratroopers were the only hope for the port of Nha Trang, but they were only a light brigade, whereas the enemy facing them consisted of at least a division, supported by many heavy tanks, long-range cannon and intense antiaircraft. On our side there remained no tanks and only a few 105s and 155s.

"After a week of hard and unequal combat" and after suffering heavy casualties, the Airborne brigade was finally outflanked and its few survivors withdrew down Route 21 toward Nha Trang. Their withdrawal in turn precipitated the sudden evacuation of several ARVN training centers situated on the road:

> Along the road from Ban Me Thuot to Nha Trang we had two or three training centers, so when the Airborne withdrew along the road, all these training centers just disbanded and ran with the Airborne. When the Airborne and these troops ran out of the camp, and Nha Trang knew about this, then Nha Trang ran too. If we had had responsible people to hold Nha Trang and to organize a defense of Nha Trang, I think that we could hold it for a while.[18]

Nha Trang was, by this time, near chaos. According to a general officer stationed there at the time, "the flow of civilian refugees and military evacuees from I Corps area and from the neighboring provinces created an atmosphere of panic and of hysteria which soon became uncontrollable. A further evacuation from Nha Trang was initiated by individual units without orders or coordination with Corps headquarters which was then completely paralyzed and overwhelmed by the situation." Even though there were still Regional Forces, Popular Forces, and some ARVN forces in the Nha Trang area (including the 40th regiment of the 22nd Division), all command and control rapidly evaporated. There was, in the words of Colonel Ly, "no support, no command, how can they fight?"

On April 1, "the Corps staff at Nha Trang began to flee, people disappeared," among them General Phu, the II Corps Commander. Colonel Ly recalled vividly his commander's departure:

[18] Colonel Loi's account of the domino effect caused by the Airborne withdrawal typifies the problems ARVN had in mounting a sustained defense in any particular area during the final weeks.

I had a visit from Phu about noon time. He came back to headquarters and said, "Where are the people?" I was in my office upstairs and he kept yelling, and I said, "I'm still here, working here. I think they must have taken the noon break." The key officers were still here but Phu left the headquarters and he walked to the helipad just in front of his house, next to the headquarters and he left. Later on I learned that he had flown to Saigon. Of course, when the key staff officers saw him leaving, they also left. [It was the] first of April. Again, the second time, I was left behind. Without any orders. I didn't know what happened, what was going on. I was alone with my aide, my secretary and some junior officers and Phu's security officer. A Ranger major who commanded troops to secure Phu's house was also left behind. I called the Ranger officer, and with some Rangers, we hit the airfield. I met my staff there. They were already there, they had seen Phu leave. I tried to gather them in the airport and talk with the Air Division Commander. The Air Force personnel tried to hold us as hostages in order to call Phu back, because the Air Force needed infantry troops to protect their base. They tried to hold us, but I said, we have no way to contact Phu now. And they tried to contact Saigon, and General Vien said, "Phu must stay there to defend effectively Nha Trang. Don't withdraw anymore." But who obeyed orders? All the troops abandoned their posts. No fighting at all. Panic in Nha Trang and every city in II Corps at that time. By eight o'clock in the evening the last airplane (I think) took me to Saigon.

With the departure of all senior commanders, "everyone ran." There was

. . . no one in charge of the whole area. So everyone is thinking about running. That is all. Each province chief is in charge of a big sum of money, so everyone tries to get it out from the treasury and run with it.

Thus, with the exception of the two southeastern provinces of II Corps (Ninh Thuan and Binh Thuan), where the GVN still retained a tenuous hold, the Communists were in control of both the highlands and the coastal areas by the beginning of April.

Chapter 13

The Fall of I Corps

The Fall of I Corps

Because of its proximity to the DMZ, its unfavorable terrain, and the sizable Communist forces in the area, I Corps had the largest concentration of GVN strength of any Corps area. As of March 1, there were five divisions, including South Vietnam's major reserve units, the Marines and Airborne, one armored brigade, four Ranger groups, plus some 220 Regional Force companies.[19] The opposing Communist forces in early March were equivalent to some seven divisions, but, as the I Corps Commander, General Truong, pointed out, there were also several additional NVA reserve divisions above the DMZ which could be inserted rapidly into the I Corps area.

The defenders in I Corps faced a difficult tactical challenge. In order to protect the major population centers in the coastal lowlands and the logistic route connecting them (Route 1), it was necessary for the GVN to hold the key terrain features and ridge lines immediately west of the lowland areas. But such a defense had been greatly complicated by the substantial improvements the Communists had made in their lines of communication since the Paris Agreements. This series of roads permitted the Communists to maneuver and supply their forces at a number of points in close

---

[19] As reported by Colonel Dang, the I Corps Chief of Staff. Running from north to south, I Corps' regular divisions were deployed as follows: the Marine Division in Quang Tri; the 1st Division in Thua Thien; the Airborne Division in Quang Nam, mostly southwest of Danang; the 3rd Division in Quang Nam, mostly southwest of Danang; and the 2nd Division in Quang Tin and Quang Ngai.

proximity to these lowland areas and provided them with jumping-off positions from which to launch armored assaults with little or no warning.

The heavy concentration of GVN forces in I Corps was also a reflection of the intensity of the fighting in that area. During 1974, I Corps had been the scene of a series of Communist assaults which had cost the GVN more than 15,000 casualties to repulse. Fighting had been particularly severe in Quang Nam province, where the Communists had mounted an attack in midsummer which gravely threatened the Danang area. This offensive had been stemmed only after heavy fighting by the 3rd Division, reinforced by two brigades of the Airborne and several Ranger units.

Later in the year, the Communists opened an attack on a key terrain feature (Nui Mo Tau) some 15 miles southwest of Hue. After fighting which seesawed back and forth over several months, the Communists succeeded in capturing this high ground toward the end of the year. Forward observation posts on Nui Mo Tau allowed them to adjust their 122mm rocket and 122mm and 130mm artillery fire on the 1st Division headquarters and airfield near Hue. This artillery harassment forced the closing of the airport which, in the words of the 1st Division's Deputy Commander, Colonel Thuc, had a "great psychological effect" on the people. "The wealthy people of Hue and Quang Tri packed up and moved to the south. The government officials and officers of VNAF also evacuated their families to Danang and other safe cities." Despite repeated attacks, bad weather (which inhibited air strikes and degraded the accuracy of artillery fire) and restrictions on "mortar and artillery ammunition" prevented the GVN from reoccupying this position until January 10.

Communist prisoners captured during the battle for Nui Mo Tau reported that they had been instructed to hold this position until after Tet, when it would serve as the jumping-off line for a major assault on Hue. Other indications of an impending Communist offensive were also in evidence. According to one senior I Corps commander, air reconnaissance had detected a "dramatic" increase in Communist logistical activities during the later part of 1974. It was estimated that the Communists were bringing "some

10,000 tons of supplies (mostly ammunition and food)'' into I Corps every month.

On February 17, an air observer spotted "a big enemy convoy of 100 trucks" moving toward a ridge line some 28 miles southwest of Hue. Several new field artillery positions were identified in the area, along with bulldozers building new roads toward friendly positions. However, I Corps headquarters failed to act on this intelligence and would not authorize artillery fire on these new positions.

On March 8, the NVA 324th Division (reinforced by two independent regiments) launched a "powerful assault on the chain of high grounds which controlled the key Phu Bai logistical installations and airport" situated near Route 1 south of Hue. At the same time, the Communists also launched attacks in the "Street Without Joy" area north of Hue and infiltrated five battalions into the coastal plains of Quang Tri and Thua Thien in order to attack the GVN's infrastructure in these provinces. However, a vigorous defense by Marine, 1st Division, and local units was able to beat back these attacks, which reportedly cost the VC and NVA over 1,000 killed. Simultaneously with these attacks in the north, the Communists also opened an offensive in the southern region of I Corps. On March 10 they started to attack a number of remote towns in Quang Tin province, including two district seats (Han Duc and Tien Phuoc) which were situated on the approach route to Tam Ky, the capital of Quang Tin province. Although the Communists succeeded in overrunning the two district towns and were able to bring Tam Ky under artillery fire, the ARVN 2nd Division succeeded in preventing further incursions.

While I Corps was able to contain these initial assaults, the situation began to deteriorate within a matter of days. Two events occurred simultaneously which were to have catastrophic consequences for the GVN's defensive posture in the area. These were the realignment of forces, which I Corps initiated to accommodate the previously ordered withdrawal of the Airborne Division, and the news of the loss of Ban Me Thuot and the retreat from Pleiku and Kontum.

As noted earlier, I Corps had been directed on March 10 to begin

209

the withdrawal of the Airborne back to Saigon.[20] Initially, I Corps had hoped to phase in the withdrawal gradually, but Saigon, concerned about the situation in II Corps and the continued Communist pressure in III Corps, demanded that the movements be speeded up by several days. Two of the three Marine brigades in Quang Tri were moved down to Quang Nam to defend the area formerly secured by the Airborne. Commenting on this pressure to advance the time frame of the redeployment, General Truong reported that Saigon had "pushed to get it back." It was "not the time to do it," and the soldiers were very jumpy when they learned from BBC broadcasts what had happened at Ban Me Thuot.[21] As a result, General Truong was forced to "hurry the Marines from their position in Quang Tri down to the Danang area." The people became very "frightened" when they observed the rapidity of these force movements.

The respondents pointed to the withdrawal of the Airborne and the repositioning of forces as having had a critical impact on subsequent events in I Corps. In the words of the Corps' Chief of Staff, Colonel Dang, "this had three bad effects. It reduced our fighting strength; it reduced the morale of our troops; and it hurt the morale of the population. It upset the balance of forces." The "balance of forces" was indeed disturbed, as I Corps Forward

[20] Interview with General Truong.

[21] Almost every soldier in the Vietnamese army had a radio receiver in order to keep posted on the situation, and many listened to the BBC, believing it more credible than the government radio. Several respondents were highly critical of BBC broadcasts during the period of the collapse, charging that they were inaccurate and biased in favor of the enemy. For example, the Commander of the Artillery Command, General Thinh, stated:

Aside from the effects of the Communists' propaganda rumor, there also was the negative influence of transmissions in Vietnamese by the BBC. It is well-known that in Vietnam the people preferred to listen to the BBC or the VOA to news by Radio Saigon because Radio Saigon was controlled by the government. During the two last months of war in Vietnam, it seemed that the BBC was in favor of the Communists in its commentaries or in its daily news. When Nha Trang or Phan Rang were still under Vietnamese control, the BBC already announced the fall of these cities. When the Vietnamese advance units were at the level of Phan Rang and the South Vietnamese government was trying to negotiate with the North, the BBC said that the only possible aim of these negotiations could be the surrender of South Vietnam.

now had only the 1st Infantry Division, one Marine brigade, and two "depleted" Ranger groups to face an enemy of four infantry divisions, and the defenses of Quang Nam had also been weakened.

But even more important, these redeployments had a major, adverse psychological impact. The Marines and Airborne had "provided a sense of security" to the people in their respective areas. The people of Quang Nam "trusted the Airborne" because of its role in stopping the Communist drive on Danang the year before, and the Marines were held in similar esteem by the population of Quang Tri. As Buu Vien put it:

> In the minds of the people of Quang Tri and Hue the presence of these two divisions was so essential to the security of the area that the news of the withdrawal of the Airborne Division completely confounded them.

The Chief of Staff of I Corps described the situation as follows:

> When we took the Marines out of Quang Tri, it upset the population there so when we withdrew the Marines to replace the Airborne, we had the same effect in Quang Tri as we had had withdrawing the Airborne from Quang Nam. The people and the soldiers got upset. As soon as we started to withdraw the Marines from Quang Tri the collapse started already. They went down by truck over Highway 1.

As noted above, the repositioning of forces triggered a flow of refugees from the northern provinces. In the words of one senior commander, "with the departure of the Marine Division from the northern provinces the civilian population began to panic and evacuate en masse Quang Tri and Hue."

A major underlying reason for the panic was a belief among the population that a "deal" had been made concerning a further division of South Vietnam—that I Corps was to be abandoned to the Communists. Rumors concerning a possible new division of South Vietnam had been prevalent for some time in I Corps. According to Buu Vien:

211

Ever since the 1972 Communist offensive, the people in the north-ernmost provinces of South Vietnam lived in constant fear of being abandoned to the Communists. When the Paris talks resumed there were rumors that a cession of the northern provinces in exchange for complete withdrawal of North Vietnamese troops might be possible, and there was also speculation of a coalition government in Saigon and the creation of a buffer state in central Vietnam under ex-Emperor Bao Dai. Amid those rumors and speculation, there was a steady movement to the south by wealthy businessmen and those people who have enough possessions to establish a new life in Saigon.[22]

Aware of these concerns, the GVN had attempted to "allay the fear of the people" by maintaining the two ARVN elite divisions in the northern Corps and by earmarking government funds for development programs in the Danang and Hue areas.

With the departure of the Airborne, the rumors of a "deal" were rekindled and quickly spread among both the civilian population and the military forces, including the officer corps. They were given further credibility when word was received of the loss of Ban Me Thuot and the withdrawal from Pleiku and Kontum. Buu Vien continued:

. . . the retreat from Kontum and Pleiku had dealt a serious blow to the morale of the troops in MR I. Rumors of a deal between the government and the Communists spread like wildfire among the soldiers. It was not known where the rumors had originated, but instinct led the soldiers to believe that an agreement had been reached by the two sides for another partition of the country, a solution that time and again many people had been talking about. Furthermore, the retreat from Kontum and Pleiku was so sudden and so brusque, so without any fighting, that there seemed to be no other explanation.

To make matters worse, the GVN apparently made no attempt to counter these rumors. This led even high-ranking officers to

[22] Respondents reported that rumors of a "deal" to further partition South Vietnam were also prevalent in II Corps and contributed to the demoralization of forces in that area as well.

believe the United States had agreed to a new partition line. Commenting on the importance of this governmental passiveness, one general officer stated:

> Rumors, as a matter of fact, were very important for the morale of the troops and the population as well. In Vietnam, in the closing days of the war, people talked about secret agreements between the U.S. and the NVA concerning the partition of South Vietnam along certain lines. Curiously, the government information agencies as well as the Army Directorate of Psychological Warfare never denied these rumors. The officers and soldiers asked themselves: "Why do we have to fight to defend Danang when it had been agreed that the new demarcation line [will be from Ban Me Thuot to Phan Rang]?"

Other respondents were also puzzled by and critical of the fact that the government did nothing during the course of the collapse to reassure the people of I Corps. In the words of Buu Vien:

> While the country was plunged in unprecedented turmoil and on the verge of collapse, the government adopted a strange attitude, a silence that was hard to understand except for a few appearances on TV and radio by President Thieu. People asked themselves questions and they tried to answer them themselves. Rumors circulated in place of government announcements. The Ministry of Information was mute, because the Minister himself didn't know much about the situation and didn't know what the President's intention was. Furthermore, he didn't dare to take the initiative and talk about things the President might not like or agree with. Since the resignation of Hoang Duc Nha as Minister of Information, information activities seemed to go at a slow pace. Nha, as cousin of the President, was the only Minister who had direct access to the President, and as a result of his closeness to the President, could have come up with daring initiative and quick reaction to the development.

An underlying motivation spurring the flight of the population was the fear of Communist repression should they fall into enemy hands. This fear was inflamed by the memory of Communist

213

atrocities in Hue during its occupation at the time of the 1968 Tet offensive. Again, to quote Buu Vien:

> The Communist massacre of the Hue people in 1968 also contributed to the enemy's success in 1975. Nobody, especially the people of Hue, ever forgot the tragic days of the 1968 Tet attack when thousands of civilians were induced to attend Communist indoctrination courses and [were] later found executed in cold blood by the Communists. Nobody ever forgot that long search for their children, relatives who were supposed to have been attending classes somewhere in the area, only to find them buried in mass graves, with their skulls crushed and their hands tied behind their backs. The specter of that horrible slaughter was revived vividly in the people's memory and hardly anybody, especially those who had close or distant connections with the nationalist government, dared to stay behind. The fear of Communist persecution was one of the main factors that prompted the exodus of hundreds of thousands of refugees to Danang.[23]

Driven by these fears, the people continued to accelerate their movement out of Quang Tri and Thua Thien. This had several pernicious effects: It clogged roads and impeded GVN military movements; it underminded the cohesion of the fighting forces because of concern for the welfare of their dependents; and it eventually burdened the city of Danang with two million refugees, which doomed any successful defense of that enclave.

Concerned about the growing number of refugees on his lines of communication, General Truong called Prime Minister Khiem in Saigon and told him that I Corps had increasing reservations about its ability to execute the withdrawal of forces into Danang that was directed in President Thieu's orders of March 13. Khiem, accompanied by some other cabinet members, flew to Danang on March 18 and met with General Truong, along with mayors, province

---

[23] According to Buu Vien, the Communists "intensified" their propaganda efforts to encourage this fear. "In addition to urging mutiny and desertion and promising clemency to those who 'repent and return to the right path of revolution,' their efforts concentrated on creating extreme fear among the population and refugees in the city of Danang."

chiefs, and other high officials from the I Corps area. These local administrative officials, said Buu Vien, pressed the Prime Minister

> . . . with questions as to whether or not they were authorized now to evacuate the civilian population, especially the dependents of government officials, cadres and soldiers. Prime Minister Khiem didn't answer the question directly, but decided that a high-level government delegation headed by a Deputy Prime Minister would be established and stationed in Danang to help take care of the refugee problem. The Minister of Public Works and Transportation was directed to help charter and requisition ships and boats necessary for transportation.

However, Buu Vien stated that this plan was not carried out, as "no high-level government delegation was sent to Danang" to help with the refugee coordination task. Moreover, even though the GVN set about acquiring bottoms for the evacuation of refugees, it appears that few if any of these ships were ever actually sent to I Corps. As one respondent put it, "They had confiscated all the ships in Saigon to evacuate them but . . . did nothing." Meanwhile, various government officials and their families in Quang Tri and Thua Thien joined the movement of refugees to Danang, as did the dependents of the ARVN 1st Division.

On the morning of March 19, the I Corps Commander was ordered back to Saigon to review his plans for the redeployment of Danang. At a meeting in the Palace, General Truong repeated to President Thieu and General Vien what he had told Prime Minister Khiem on the previous day about the situation developing in I Corps—the movement of refugees, the role of rumors, and the effect the withdrawal of the Airborne was having on the morale of the people.[24] He outlined the tentative plan he had developed for the redeployment to Danang but pointed out that the enemy was already exerting strong pressure on his lines of communication and the situation was changing almost daily. After offering the judg-

[24] This account of the March 19 meeting was derived from an interview with General Truong.

ment that a withdrawal from Hue to Danang no longer appeared practical because of the mass of refugees on Route 1, General Truong suggested that the best way to deal with the situation at that moment was to "stay in Hue and fight." He said this might give the population some "confidence" and argued that he had "good defensive positions around Hue." He went on to propose that he regroup his forces into three enclaves, Hue, Danang, and Chu Lai. Both President Thieu and General Vien approved the field commander's plan.

During the course of the meeting, General Truong also raised the question of Saigon's intentions vis-à-vis the Marine Division stationed in I Corps. He told the President that he had heard a rumor that Saigon would also withdraw this force. He said he was "not curious, but he needed to know for his own planning." President Thieu responded that there were no plans to move the Marines and that they would "stay in I Corps." He further told General Truong that he could "keep Hue" and protect as much of I Corps as possible but that the withdrawal of the Airborne elements would continue. After hearing this new decision, General Truong reported he "felt good." However, following the meeting, he had lunch with Prime Minister Khiem and asked him privately about the status of the Marines. The Prime Minister disclosed that there were indeed plans under way to bring back the Marines. Upon learning this, General Truong said, his spirits were "crushed."

During the night of March 19, NVA infantry supported by armored elements launched a frontal attack on the Regional Forces now guarding the northern section of Quang Tri, forcing these units to retreat to the My Chanh River. The next morning, General Truong flew to meet with the commanders of I Corps Forward and informed them of the President's decision to "hold" Hue. He received a "confident" response to this plan from the commanders, who seemed "to have a good spirit."[25] When General Truong returned to Danang on the evening of March 20, however, he was met by startling new instructions from the JGS, which he

[25] The new policy to hold Hue was confirmed the afternoon of March 20, when President Thieu announced over the radio that South Vietnamese forces intended to defend Hue "at any price."

interpreted as orders to abandon Hue.[26] The message, as General Truong recalled, stated that the JGS had "means to supply only one enclave in I Corps" and that plans should be made to withdraw to Danang when I Corps considered such a redeployment possible.[27]

While General Truong understood the message as clearly ordering a withdrawal to Danang, this apparently was not the thrust intended by the JGS. According to the General Staff officer who drafted the message, it was only meant to warn the I Corps Commander that Saigon had insufficient resources to support three enclaves at one time and to give him the discretion to withdraw to Danang should the military situation worsen and require such action. However, even this officer agreed that at best the text was "ambiguous." This misunderstanding was but one manifestation of the serious problems in communication and coordination that existed between the I Corps and Saigon staffs. The JGS did not appear to comprehend the gravity of the situation in I Corps, which it felt was being "exaggerated" by local commanders there. One JGS officer complained of "inadequate" and "inaccurate" reporting from I Corps, while General Truong, on the other hand, faulted the "weak" planning support and command from Saigon. He commented that when the Americans had been in Vietnam, I Corps could rely on U.S. channels. However, with the departure of U.S. forces, coordination was no longer "appropriate to deal with the situation."

The need for a firm decision vis-à-vis the defense of Hue became apparent as the military situation in I Corps Forward rapidly worsened. On March 20, two NVA divisions, the 324th and 325th, launched a coordinated attack on the 1st Division and Ranger units in the Phu Loc area south of Hue and threatened to cut Route 1 between Hue and Danang. Despite intensive close air support and a determined counterattack by a Marine battalion rushed to the area, GVN forces were unable to reoccupy the high

---

[26] The message had been flown up from Saigon by special courier.

[27] General Truong said he was so stunned by this change of orders that he called his deputy over and said, "Read this for me."

ground seized by the enemy and were soon forced to retreat. Describing these events, a high-ranking I Corps officer stated:

> The 15th Ranger group, despite an heroic defense, was overrun by the 325th NVA Division on March 21st. The strategic Mom Cum Sat mountain which controlled Highway 1, south of Truoi, was lost and Hue was cut off from Danang. On the 22nd, the 1st Infantry Division had to blow up the Truoi bridge. In the afternoon, under heavy pressure, it had to withdraw to Phu Bai where hand-to-hand combat took place during the night.

At the same time, GVN forces defending north of Hue began to be pushed back toward the city, which was now threatened with envelopment. Moreover, the cohesion of the South Vietnamese forces began to give way. The I Corps Chief of Staff stated that "everything was out of control" and that the commanders "reported back that they could not control their troops, that the troops deserted, that they did not have enough supplies and that they could not control the situation. They reported that they had to abandon Hue."

Faced with this deteriorating situation, General Truong, on March 25, requested that plans be prepared for the withdrawal of troops from I Corps Forward and that evening ordered the evacuation of Hue.[28] Colonel Thuc recalled how the Commander of the 1st Division presented the decision to his staff:

> He came to the meeting room with a sad and uneasy voice, saying, "We've been *betrayed! We have to abandon Hue,* the loveliest part of South Vietnam. . . . The purpose of the Hue abandonment is: save our forces. It now is "sauve qui peut" ("every man for himself"). Anyone may go down to the seashore, just walk along it to Danang and the VN Navy will pick up anyone who gets sick or tired of walking on the sand. The rally point: south of the Hai Van Pass. Good luck to you all and see you in Danang." He added, "Keep quiet while withdrawing, no radio will be turned on."

The withdrawal plan approved by General Truong envisaged

[28] General Truong stated that he received another message from the JGS around March 25 which again ordered him to redeploy all his forces in I Corps to defend Danang and instructed him to send the Marines back to Saigon.

that a portion of the troops in I Corps Forward would be evacuated by sea at the Thuan An inlet north of Hue, while the remainder would march to the Cau Tu Hien inlet (at Dam Cau Hai) southeast of Hue. The Navy had promised to sink some boats across the shallow tidal basin at Cau Tu Hien in order to provide a bridge across the inlet, and the Marines were ordered to secure the high ground immediately south of the inlet (Hui Vinh Phong) to protect the crossing.

Unfortunately, the withdrawal turned out to be a "costly failure," as neither the Navy nor the Marines carried out their missions. The Navy failed to sink the required boats, and many 1st Division soldiers were drowned at Cau Tu Hien in the rising tide; many more were later shot down by NVA elements from Hui Vinh Phong, which was supposed to have been secured by the Marines. Furthermore, command over the withdrawing troops was inadequate and, in the words of General Truong, there was "not good discipline." As another former I Corps commander put it:

> There was a French saying, "Hell was paved with good intentions," of which Cau Tu Hien was a stirring illustration.

The withdrawal by sea at Thuan An to the north did not go much better. The Navy ships were late in arriving, and strong seas prevented them from taking more than half of the waiting troops. All the armor and other equipment had to be left behind, and enemy shelling disrupted operations, causing many casualties. All told, less than half of the troops scheduled for evacuation from I Corps Forward arrived in Danang, and those that did make their way there were completely disorganized.[29] Upon arriving in

[29] Some local units in I Corps Forward apparently were not even informed of the withdrawal order. General Don reported that the District Chief of Huong Tra, near Hue, told him that he had received no orders at all. Commanding some 3,000 Regional and Popular Forces, the District Chief, who held the rank of colonel, was surprised one morning that he had no communication with his superiors and drove to the Province Chief's headquarters where he didn't see anyone: "I asked about the generals—no more generals—all these leaders had left the post in the night, and they didn't say anything to anyone." He encountered a regimental commander of the 1st Division and asked him what had happened. The commander replied, "Oh, there are no more leaders now." He said, "You are commander of this place."

Danang, the 1st Infantry remnants dispersed trying to find their dependents and as a result were no longer of fighting value.

Hue's abandonment apparently came as a surprise to President Thieu. Upon hearing the news, Thieu called Truong to confirm it and asked the I Corps Commander, "If I order you back to Hue, can you do it?" General Truong is reported by a JGS officer to have responded, "If you order me, I could do it, but I'm not sure how long I could defend."

At the same time General Truong was attempting to execute the withdrawal from Hue, the situation suddenly collapsed in the southern sector of I Corps. On March 24, "after crashing through the defense lines of the 5th Regiment, 2nd Division, one NVA armored column, in a daring raid, took the capital city of Tam Ky by surprise." This cut Route 1 between Chu Lai and Danang and sealed off southern I Corps. The Communists also began to surround Quang Ngai city, and during the night of March 25, Quang Ngai sector attempted to withdraw by land to Chu Lai. This maneuver was not successful, however, because the enemy was strongly emplaced between Quang Ngai and Chu Lai and only a few units managed to get through. The 2nd Division was also forced to withdraw to Chu Lai, where, surrounded and disorganized, it was ordered evacuated by ship to the island of Cu Lao Re, some 20 miles offshore. Only a portion of the 2nd Division's force could be extracted, however, and only about 2,000 troops from this division were eventually brought down to the Saigon area.

With the collapse of the northern and southern fronts of I Corps, its defensive forces were now reduced to the 3rd Division, two Marine brigades, and various Regional and Popular units still resisting in the Danang area. These were soon confronted by an enemy force of almost five divisions.[30] Moreover, behind this thin defensive line, the rear base of Danang was rapidly moving toward chaos. As more and more refugees poured into the city, govern-

[30] Threatening them from the west were the Communist 304th and 311th Divisions, along with units from the 44th Front. Pressure was also being exerted from the south by the 52nd Brigade and from the north by elements of the 325th and 324th NVA Divisions.

ment control began to break down, partly due to the lack of adequate police. Realizing the situation was becoming unmanageable, and unwilling to stop the flow of refugees for humanitarian reasons,[31] General Truong urgently requested assistance from Saigon, both for transportation to move the refugees out of Danang and for food and other vital provisions. However, except for a few transport flights, no help was forthcoming.[32] In General Truong's words, Saigon was "silent on the refugee problem," and the people "saw no encouraging response from the government."

Danang soon contained an estimated two million persons, including many GVN soldiers,[33] and with food reserves running out, looting became commonplace. Panic set in, with the rich, civil servants, and police, among others, desperately trying to evacuate their families. Describing this chaotic situation, a high-ranking officer from I Corps recalled:

> . . . Danang, now overcrowded with two million refugees from Quang Tri, Hue, and Quang Tin, was practically under siege. The population began to panic when they saw the evacuation of U.S. personnel and Vietnamese employees from the U.S. Consulate General. People were fighting to board commercial and American ships to flee the city. The airport was invaded, even military aircraft were seized and could not take off. Remnants of defeated

[31] Checkpoints had been set up outside Danang around March 17 or 18 to control the flow of refugees, but they proved impractical, as any slowdown caused the columns to back up and created disorder as far north as the Hai Van Pass. Since the Communists were shelling the refugee columns, General Truong said he could not stop their movement, for "humanitarian reasons." The 3rd Division Commander, General Hinh, also pointed out that had the refugees been prevented from passing through the GVN lines around Danang, the defending units would have been impeded by the mass of humanity directly in front of their positions. However, he also felt that the overriding consideration was that the GVN had always thought in terms of getting the civilian population on its side and therefore could not "reject its own people."

[32] Air Vietnam was instructed to increase its flights to Danang, but, according to Buu Vien, "flights were often interrupted and planes returned to Saigon empty because landing in Danang was impossible due to the frantic and panicky situation of refugees at the airport."

[33] The ARVN 3rd Division Commander reported that VC sapper units were also in the city, which contributed to the chaotic conditions.

units falling back on Danang and refugees coming from overrun district towns helped spread panic and disorder with any imaginable kind of rumor. . . . Bands of children, hungry and thirsty, wandered aimlessly on the streets, demolishing everything which happened to fall into their hands. Danang was seized by the convulsions of collective hysteria.

While some soldiers "were still fighting well," increasing numbers of desertions began to occur in both enlisted and officer ranks. One general, who visited the 2nd Regiment of the 3rd Division on March 27, reported finding that some "officers had left their units and came back to Danang, trying to send their families off to Saigon." He continued:

I left the 2nd Regiment and flew to Dai Loc district town, but as we were approaching the town, I was warned by Corps Tactical Operations Center (TOC) that the town was now under enemy control. Later, I was informed that the RFs just left the district without a fight to go back to Danang and take care of their families. The same thing happened to the Danang ammunition depot where two RF companies just disappeared.

Desertions eventually spread to even Truong's headquarters. His Chief of Staff, Colonel Dang, reported that:

. . . even at I Corps headquarters, the men deserted. Our drivers, our communication people, men from the headquarters companies, they deserted.[34]

On March 28, General Truong received information from Saigon that the Communists were concentrating their forces for a major attack against Danang the next day. At the same time, the NVA started heavily shelling the air and naval bases at Danang and the "civilian mass" compressed within the city. Considering the situation to be "hopeless," General Truong said he called Pres-

[34] General Truong told Tran Van Don he was "alone" in his command post at the very end. Don said, "When he came to find his people, his staff, he said nobody was there. He was alone. No soldiers, not even soldiers."

ident Thieu and requested permission to withdraw his remaining forces from Danang. Thieu, however, equivocated and would not "make any clear decision." Communications were soon cut by artillery fire and General Truong made the decision on his own to withdraw.[35]

The evacuation on March 29 was not successful; in General Truong's words, "not many got out." Only about 6,000 Marines (45 percent of the Division) and 4,000 other assorted troops succeeded in reaching Navy ships and civilian craft. The Marine evacuation was the most successful because the Marines were, for the most part, "under good control" and were the Navy's "top priority." The 3rd Division fared the least well: Of its original 12,000 men, only 5,000 reached the embarkation point,[36] and, according to its commander, General Hinh, only about 1,000 of these could be evacuated on the single ship available there. When asked why the evacuation had gone so badly, General Truong responded, "We did not have a plan for withdrawal [and had to] use what was on hand." It was a "reaction of the moment" and not well organized.

Indeed, in many instances there was no organization or command at all. As one senior officer described it:

> Some Marine stragglers mixed up with the population and boarded civilian barges and commercial ships. Frustrated, hungry, and leaderless, they went wild and some of them indulged in inadmissible acts of banditry. Billions of dollars of equipment were destroyed and left to the enemy. Thus fell the second biggest city of

[35] Thieu eventually did come to a decision, after the withdrawal was already under way; the decision was transmitted through Navy channels to the Naval Task Force off Danang. A high-ranking officer, who was aboard ship at the time, was presented with the message from the JGS "stating that according to Presidential instructions the order to defend Danang was still valid." The officer commented, "At that time, the evacuation of the Marine Division was almost complete and [the] NVA had already occupied the city of Danang. Either Saigon was completely in the dark or the message was just for the historical record."

[36] According to General Hinh, most of the 3rd Division troops deserted during the course of the withdrawal to the sea in an attempt to rescue their dependents in Danang. However, their families were no longer at their homes and the troops could not locate them in the seething morass of population.

Vietnam. She had gone through a stage of insanity before she died of suffocation.

General Truong, whom some of our respondents considered an "able" and "honest" officer, said that the collapse of I Corps was fundamentally the result of a "disadvantageous" balance of forces. In his view, a sustained defense was "impossible" with the forces at hand. He contended that he would have required at least two additional divisions to have "held" against those NVA units already operating in I Corps in March, not to mention the additional Communist reserves across the DMZ. Thus the withdrawal of the Airborne placed an intolerable strain on a defense posture that was already inadequate.[37] Indeed, General Truong suggested that he would have lost Danang in 1974 without the Airborne, and even with them, he would have had great difficulty "stabilizing" the situation had the Communists chosen to launch a general offensive throughout I Corps in that year.

To emphasize the magnitude of the military problems confronting I Corps in 1975, General Truong compared that situation with the Easter offensive of 1972: In 1972, the Communists had to launch their armored drives from north of the DMZ and as a result had to "maneuver" their mechanized units over considerable distances before they could attack major GVN population centers. In 1975, however, the NVA, using the numerous feeder roads they had built, could start their armored and other forces from close in and could rapidly attack fixed GVN positions throughout the Corps area. Communist firepower was also much stronger than it had been in 1972, as they now possessed the capability to deliver massed artillery fire with great effect even on well-fortified and dug-in GVN positions.

The major difference between 1975 and 1972, however, was the absence of U.S. air support, which had played a decisive role in arresting the earlier Communist drive. In 1972, I Corps had averaged some 260 tactical air and 25 B-52 sorties daily, whereas in

[37] General Truong stated that had the Airborne not been withdrawn the situation would have been "much better," but he still would not have had adequate forces to hold against a general offensive.

1975, VNAF could mount less than 50 sorties a day.[38] General Truong contended that "without B-52s, it was difficult to stop the enemy" and that he could have "contained" the 1975 offensive had he been able to call upon the U.S. air support that was available in 1972.

Another former I Corps general also stressed the importance of U.S. air support, particularly B-52s, in the defeat of the 1972 Communist offensive and pointed to a change in naval fire support as well:

> . . . Whereas in 1972 the American 7th Fleet could provide massive area fire up to 20 km inland, in 1975 the naval fire support was practically nil. The entire Vietnamese Navy had five old destroyers whose guns could reach targets only from five to seven km inland.

Noting other critical changes in ARVN's capabilities since 1972, the general went on:

> The combat and combat support units were acutely short in artillery and mortar ammunition. While in 1972 we could shoot an unlimited number of artillery rounds, . . . in 1975 the available supply rate . . . was less than ten percent of what we fired in 1972.
>
> While the combat units badly needed ammunition, the service units were acutely short of POL . . . and spare parts. Due to the lack of gasoline, the air force had to ground many types of aircraft. . . . The helicopters available for troop transportation and supplies were also critically reduced. In MR I in 1975 we could barely move by helicopter one infantry company at one time. . . .
>
> The artillery units were short of trucks and even prime movers to tow guns and I knew of no one artillery battery in MR I capable of carrying its basic load of ammunition. . . . The transportation units experienced the same shortage of trucks and POL. Whereas in

[38] General Truong put the average number of VNAF sorties at 30 to 40 a day in March. However, the respondents differed in their opinions of the effectiveness of VNAF during the last weeks. General Truong thought they gave "very good support," particularly at Phu Loc, whereas his Chief of Staff characterized them as "terrible. . . . They were not effective. They always went at such high altitude and did not hit anything. They were afraid of the enemy antiaircraft."

1972 we could move at will any units from one area to another (for instance, the Airborne Division with two brigades were flown in from Saigon to Hue in a few days), in 1975 the shortage of trucks and POL greatly jeopardized the movement of troops and hence our strategic mobility. I Corps, for instance, didn't have in March 1975, when the situation became critical, the means to transport one single regiment, while the NVA had the capability of moving their troops at will. . . .

The one by one replacement authorized by the Paris Agreements never materialized. A tank, an Armored Personnel Carrier (APC), a truck or a bulldozer, for example, destroyed by a mine during an operation, or lost in an accident, were never replaced; and the 10th Combat Engineer Group in Danang which supported the entire MR I, had less than ten bulldozers operational in 1975. Even worse, the basic infantry weapons, the M16 rifles, were lacking in the closing months of the war. . . .

It went without saying that the lack of supplies and adequate fire support resulted in a dramatic increase in the rate of casualties. Military hospitals were overcrowded and had to double the number of beds. They were critically short of medicines, especially dextrose, antibiotics and also in plasma. (Sometimes, for instance, the shortage was so critical in Nguyen Bu Phiang General Hospital in Hue that I had to write to different pharmaceutical firms in Saigon to ask for their help.) As a result, the combat units saw their ranks rapidly depleted and were hard put replacing their losses: as a matter of fact, in 1975 no infantry battalion ever had more than 400 men available for operations, and the Ranger battalion no more than 300.

The effects of weaknesses such as those described above,[39] along with the more immediate and pernicious effects of rumor, refugee movements, and command indecision, no doubt help to explain why I Corps collapsed so rapidly and with so little combat. Aside from the initial clashes of early March and the heavy fighting around Phu Loc and Phu Bai later in the month, there

[39] General Truong, however, did not consider ammunition or other materiel shortages to have been an immediate or "big factor" in the collapse. This would have become a critical problem, in his view, only if the fighting in I Corps had continued for several months.

appear to have been no major battles of note. The I Corps Chief of Staff estimated total GVN combat losses in March to have been only between one and two thousand:

> I have to say there was no big battle. Only small engagements so the losses were not much. Maybe a thousand, maybe two thousand. But not much because no big battles.[40]

As General Truong pointed out, the troops did not have an "opportunity" to fight in most areas because of the redeployments, the mass of refugees on the lines of communication, and the breakdown in command and control. The defense had been affected by a fundamental "depression of morale."

While the I Corps commander was generally satisfied with the performance of his subordinate officers, other respondents suggested that one reason for the lack of fighting was the fact that senior officers were among the first to abandon the battlefield. Colonel Loi recalled that he had talked with "some escaped officers from I Corps who told [him] that the division commander disappeared, next the regimental commander disappeared."

> I heard that all the lower echelon battalions didn't know what they had to do. Their regimental commander just left, and they don't know where they go and no one instructed them as to what they have to do. After so many frustrating situations, no one was responsible for the whole area.

He attributed this behavior, in part, to a loss of spirit following the setbacks at Ban Me Thuot, Pleiku, and Kontum:

> This is one of the reasons. But the overall situation was hopeless. Because they knew about the aid cut; the Americans were out; Saigon was in turmoil politically; everything seemed to collapse. So, this contributed to the collapsing situation. And even the

---

[40] This was confirmed by General Hinh, who reported that the 3rd Division was never heavily engaged before its evacuation and had lost only about 50 men per regiment, compared with the Division's 1973 losses of 2,200 men and 1974 losses of 3,500 men.

decision to withdraw from Pleiku. I think that was wrong, but it just accelerated the collapsing process.

Air Marshal Ky also believed that the running out by commanders was an important factor contributing to the collapse. He portrayed a climate where "everyone watched everyone and when you see the guy next to you move . . . then you move. You run away." He related how the process of desertion had infected a helicopter unit in I Corps:

I can tell you an example of an air force pilot. With that little example we can see the whole story. That guy went to sleep after attending a meeting of all officers in the afternoon and [all] the air division commanders [had] said, we are going to stay and fight. Big meeting for all of them. So he went to sleep. About 11, he was waked up by soldiers. A soldier said, "You see, Captain, they all left," and, of course, before that, the rumor about the debacle of Ban Me Thuot and others had reached I Corps, so the pilot was waked up at about 11 that night by a soldier and he said, "They all left, what about you and me?" So he went up to the briefing room, no one [was there], but all the chiefs were packed and packing. So without asking information, without waiting for any orders, he jumped into one of the helicopters and took off south. And the others took off, and that night 26 helicopters left the base without any orders, to go south. And many ran out of gas in their hurry.

Chapter 14

The Final Month: April 1975

The Final Month: April 1975

All the respondents agreed that with the loss of I and II Corps, South Vietnam faced a precarious situation. Barring the intervention of U.S. air (particularly B-52s), most senior South Vietnamese officers saw the military situation as irretrievable. More than half of ARVN's effective fighting strength had been lost in the two northern Corps areas and this had, in the words of Buu Vien, "dealt a serious blow to the prestige and morale of the RVN armed forces because it involved the defeat of the most capable units in ARVN. It also increased the fear that U.S. abandonment of Vietnam would become a reality."

Except for the two Airborne brigades previously withdrawn from I Corps and the few units that could be reconstituted from the estimated 18,000 or so demoralized troops who had been successfully extracted from the northern Corps areas, the defense of South Vietnam now rested with the six divisions and two armored brigades and the various Ranger groups, Regional Forces, and Popular Forces organic to III and IV Corps. However, most of these indigenous units were themselves already hard pressed and tied down by local Communist forces and could not be disengaged to form reserves to meet the fresh enemy divisions moving down from the north. Of the three organic divisions responsible for the defense of III Corps, the 25th Division was situated northwest of Saigon in the Tay Ninh area, where it was being harassed by local Communist units; the 5th Division was guarding the northern approaches to the capital along Highway 13 in Binh Duong prov-

231

ince; and the 18th Division was located to the northeast at Xuan Loc, which was soon to become a major battleground. As a result of enemy pressure, these units remained more or less static for most of the month of April, and aside from guarding their immediate operational areas, provided little mutual defensive support in the final weeks.

The situation was no better in the Delta, where the three regular divisions deployed in the IV Corps area (the 7th, 9th, and 21st) also found themselves pinned down by local Communist units and thus were not available to help with the defense of III Corps or Saigon. The military balance was sufficiently critical that the IV Corps Commander, General Nam, informed the Minister of Defense that if one of his divisions was moved out he would "lose the Delta." By tying down GVN forces in IV Corps, the Communists had obviously "learned a lesson from 1972," when their forces in the Delta had remained quiet and thus allowed the GVN to reinforce III Corps from this area. But, as the Commander of the Capital Military District pointed out, "this time they tied up those troops by the activities of the local Communist forces." Aside from preventing GVN redeployments, Communist units from the IV Corps area were themselves used to bring pressure on Saigon. A number of troops were put in captured vehicles and transported to Long An province south of Saigon, where they threatened to cut Route 4, Saigon's major communication artery to the Delta, and to link up with NVA forces coming from the north to surround the capital. In order to counter this threat, the JGS reequipped the remnants of the ARVN 22nd Division, which had been evacuated from Binh Dinh, and inserted them in Long An in an attempt to keep Route 4 open. However, the 22nd Division troops numbered less than a regiment and were "in really bad shape," and eventually they became encircled.

For the immediate defense of Saigon itself, the Capital Military District had a mixed force of about two divisions. This included three Airborne battalions (which were considered "striking forces"), local Regional and Popular Forces, and a mixture of Rangers, Marines, and other troops withdrawn from I and II Corps. However, the latter were disorganized, demoralized, with-

232

out sufficient weapons, and in fact were a "contaminating factor." The general officer who was appointed Commander of the Capital Military District at the end of March, described the two Ranger brigades under his command as having "very poor cadres, insufficiently equipped" and "not wanting to fight anymore." Elaborating on the overall problem, this officer stated:

> The strength of the troops withdrawn from the highlands and assigned to me were understrength. So the government hurried to fill out their forces among the draftees and military laborers. They had no time to get fresh training and the weapons—most of them received about 50 percent of the weapons and ammunition. The morale of the cadres was very low because they had just returned from II Corps and I Corps. They were not aggressive at all. Thus, the Regional Forces and the Popular Forces are in position watching their fellow regular forces come back from the battlefield with low morale, so they didn't have any confidence about the effectiveness of those forces. And every day they learned from the refugees coming from the northern provinces, from I Corps, II Corps, many stories about the enemy so the morale of those forces was going down.

The Capital Military District Commander's assistant, Colonel Loi, corroborated the report that these troops "were in really bad shape" and "not a fighting force." The Marine units, which had become undisciplined when they withdrew from Danang, continued to present a problem when they arrived at Vung Tau, southeast of Saigon:

> When they arrived in Vung Tau no one was in charge of them. They ran to Saigon by every means, a bus, everything. So [we] had to set up a block at Thu Duc to stop all the Marines. So we got hold of the Commander of the Marines, General Lan, and had him reassemble and reequip all these people and tried to use them to defend Saigon. We reorganized one brigade of Marines, and the remaining still stayed in Vung Tau.

The situation with VNAF was hardly better. Many pilots, planes, and crews had been lost in the retreats from I and II Corps and, according to Colonel Uoc, the "operational capability of the Air Force was cut down to less than half" by early April. Air units were now restricted to the four remaining operational bases still controlled by the South Vietnamese (Phan Rang, Bien Hoa, Tan Son Nhut, and Can Tho) and there was great congestion at these facilities. Operations were limited because "pilots and mechanics were too busy taking care of their families so there were not enough people to operate them." The biggest problem was maintenance, i.e., finding persons to repair the aircraft. As Colonel Uoc described the situation:

> Every time an aircraft comes from Pleiku or somewhere else to Saigon they leave it in the open air like an air show—before the fall of Saigon, you know, 40 or 50 percent of the aircraft—helicopters, fighters, and transport planes, all kinds of aircraft—no one touched them, no one took care of them. We did not have space to deploy the aircraft—it was like a junkyard.

Against the diminished and demoralized forces of the GVN, the Communists were able to divert the numerous divisions originally targeted on I and II Corps to the final assault on III Corps and Saigon. Inasmuch as little hard fighting had taken place, these divisions were up to strength, fresh, and obviously buoyed by their enormous successes in the north. There was, however, a brief hiatus before the bulk of these NVA divisions were in position to attack III Corps. This delay was attributed to the fact that Communist commanders were caught by surprise by the sudden collapse of I and II Corps and were not postured to exploit this opportunity immediately. In the words of Colonel Loi, ". . . the Communist forces did not expect us to run like this. It took time for them to move and to reorganize." But this delay was only temporary, as Communist motorized units began to quickly flood the South Vietnamese territory north of Saigon. Toward the end of April, there were some 13 NVA divisions ringing Saigon, with another four or so held in reserve.

Given the state of their defenses and the existing balance of forces, it is understandable that the respondents had grave doubts about the GVN's ability to contain the Communist offensive. One high-ranking officer on the JGS stated that after the loss of I and II Corps he did not believe a successful defense could be mounted but nevertheless attempted as best he could to stop the Communist drive. General Truong, who was reassigned as Deputy Chairman of the JGS to work on the organization of Saigon's defenses after his evacuation from I Corps, saw that there was "no well-coordinated defensive line" around Saigon. The area was too large, the terrain too unfavorable, and not enough troops were available. The defenses were simply not sufficient to deal with a strong attack.

While pessimistic about containing the offensive with their own resources, many senior GVN officers and officials nevertheless believed that the situation still could be rescued through U.S. intervention, particularly by the resumption of B-52 bombing. Commenting on this belief, Buu Vien stated:

> The faith of the Vietnamese people in the United States was so strong that even when the Communists had occupied all the provinces and MR I and II and closed in around Saigon, there were people, including senior officials in the government, who still believed that the U.S. would soon react to drive back the Communists to save Vietnam. They believed that the U.S. was being up to something, maybe to lure the Communists into a trap to destroy once and for all their forces. It sounds naive, but it shows how strong the Vietnamese people's confidence was in the U.S.

He went on to state that "we thought that the U.S. couldn't afford losing Vietnam" because "it might lead to the eventual loss of other countries in Southeast Asia" and because "it was still in the interest of the U.S." to defend the country, having "poured in so much resources and sacrificed so many American lives." Finally, people still had faith in the "solemn pledge from the U.S. government that the U.S. would react strongly in case of Communist renewed aggression."

Agreeing that there was a prevalent belief among senior officers that American help would still be forthcoming, one high-ranking general attributed this in part to the successful assistance provided by the United States during previous military crises in South Vietnam, specifically the Tet offensive in 1968 and the Easter offensive in 1972:

> They said, we will have a third miracle. The first is Mau Tan. The Tet Mau Tan (1968), the second in 1972, and the third one will be the last. But the third one never came you see.

Even President Thieu, who had apparently ordered the redeployments in I and II Corps because he could no longer count on U.S. assistance, seems to have harbored a residual belief that American support would still be forthcoming. Tran Van Don reported that when he told Thieu on April 6 that he had reliable information from official French sources that things were "finished" for South Vietnam, Thieu responded, "I don't believe it. It is impossible that we would be abandoned by the U.S. If it would be, it would have already been in 1973."

One officer, Colonel Do Ngoc Nhan, said that even after the fall of the Cambodian capital of Phnom Penh in early April (an event which was another major psychological blow to the South Vietnamese), he and his friends still "were thinking that there was a difference between the U.S. relationship with Cambodia and that with South Vietnam":

> The U.S. only came to Cambodia because of tactical reasons which had been to defend South Vietnam and that need no longer existed. Besides, the U.S. had spent hundreds of billions of dollars on the Vietnam war, lost tens of thousands of lives there and risked its honor on the Vietnam battlefield. It would not let South Vietnam fall into the Communist hands. Having those thoughts, I looked to the U.S. and followed with concern President Ford's request of special assistance to South Vietnam in his speech to the Congress on April 16, 1975.

But others, including those who put more stock in U.S. actions, had their doubts. General Thinh recalled his disappointment at the limited number of artillery pieces and other equipment delivered by American cargo planes at Tan Son Nhut airport in April, which, in his view, constituted "only a drop of water in an arid desert and would not show the American will to continue the engagement." Air Marshal Ky was convinced that no further American support would be forthcoming and told his colleagues "again and again [there] is no way that American military forces will come back to Vietnam."

It is possible that expectations regarding American intervention were influenced by judgments about the potential efficacy of American airpower even at this late stage of the war. There were senior officers who still believed that III Corps might be defended if substantial U.S. air were available. General Thinh was most emphatic on this point: "In April 1975 they [the Communists] never could have placed their divisions around Saigon, if the U.S. had intervened with B-52s. Truly, this bomber could have changed the face of the Vietnam war." But another senior commander strongly disagreed that B-52s could have helped. The enemy had too many troops around Saigon, and the situation was beyond repair:

> Besides the three organic divisions, the 5th, 7th, 9th, they disposed seven additional divisions and an artillery division, a tank division, and many troops reinforced from I Corps, II Corps. Their whole strength, I don't know how many—more than 10 divisions. At that time I frankly tell you, no more B-52 strikes will be effective, no more aircraft because there was panic. You could shoot them, do anything you want, but no more discipline of the troops, no organization. We didn't have cadres, we lost cadres. The cadres that remained had very low morale, they lost their families, their wives, children, properties, everything. I do not believe that even B-52 strikes could have helped because it was too late. The mass of population and panic caused much trouble.

However, this seems to have been the minority view, as most of the South Vietnamese leaders still felt that U.S. air support would have been effective, and many remained convinced that the United States would resume their bombing "right up until the end."

One consequence of this prevailing faith in a last-minute U.S.

rescue may have been that at least some Vietnamese officers were discouraged from attempting to do more in their own defense. When one officer proposed to a senior commander in the JGS that action be taken to establish a rear headquarters in the IV Corps area, he was told it was "not necessary . . . because we lose the war or win the war with the intervention of the U.S. Air Force."

Whether for this reason or for others, senior civilian and military leaders in Saigon appeared, to several of the respondents, to be unable or unwilling to organize themselves for a final defense of the country. The propensity toward inaction which had characterized Saigon's role in the events of I and II Corps became even more evident as the enemy closed in. The government seemed stunned and bewildered by the fate that had befallen Vietnam and appeared unable to function. A frequent characterization of the leadership during this period was that "no one was in charge of anything." Buu Vien described President Thieu as "demoralized" and "more isolated than ever before." He also noted that "since after the fall of Ban Me Thuot, President Thieu was no longer accessible to his Ministers. He didn't hold any Council of Ministers meeting, didn't talk to the press, didn't address the National Assembly." Air Marshal Ky summed up the "atmosphere of the last few weeks" as being one where "no one was in command, no one [was] responsible for nothing."

This passiveness may be attributed in part to the uncertainties associated with changes in government. On April 4, Prime Minister Khiem resigned, and the Speaker of the House of Representatives, Can, was asked to form a new government. The political situation was further clouded by rumors of a possible coup against President Thieu. There seemed to be grounds for such speculation in that Marshal Ky, by his own admission, had begun to approach other senior officers about removing Thieu after the loss of Ban Me Thuot. While those he approached apparently agreed that Thieu should go, they were reluctant to move without American approval, which was not forthcoming. Ky reported that the officers, after checking with the Americans, had come back to him and warned "now be careful, Marshal, we don't want you to be killed by Thieu before you move. Because American officials [have] come to us and told us not to listen to Marshal Ky."

During the period prior to the formation of a new government on April 14, "the government remained more or less inactive," according to Buu Vien. Another senior official put it more strongly: ". . . between the two governments nobody worked . . . nobody took the initiative to do something." According to his own account, Can agreed to become Prime Minister because he was the only man in Thieu's camp "capable of dealing with other political and religious parties when the level of protest was disturbing the country and sapping the army's morale." He hoped that he would obtain "a sort of *modus vivendi* that would allow the armed forces to fight as long as they could." However, he asserted that "no man could have saved Vietnam at that time." An immediate priority of the new Cabinet was to relocate the hundreds of thousands of refugees who were fleeing the northern provinces in order to "prevent the uncontrolled rout from spreading hysteria in Saigon itself." This proved to be an enormous task, however, for, in the words of the Capital Military District Commander, "the problem of the refugees increased daily. We didn't have enough camps to set them up. Most of them were sent from the coastal regions by boat and instead of locating them away from the capital, they penetrated the city and became disorganized, and the people living in the cities were afraid."

Upon taking office, the new Minister of Defense in the Can Cabinet, General Don, persuaded Thieu to place under "house arrest" about a dozen generals and province chiefs pending an investigation of their role in the collapse of I and II Corps.[41] Don requested this action "to show the Army that we would like to stop the Communists" and "can be very firm, very hard." After making a tour of the battlefields, Don also met with his senior generals and tried to impress upon them the importance of containing the military situation if a political solution was to be found:

---

[41] The most notable exception was General Truong, the former I Corps Commander, who was given a new assignment with the JGS.

239

I said to the generals, I met with them three times, I said to them even if we have a political solution, a cease-fire, we need on this side to hold the military situation. We cannot talk, we cannot discuss with the other side, if we lose completely the military situation. And I told these people, these generals, including the Chief of the General Staff and he agreed with me. He said, yes, you are right. It is the first time somebody talked to us like this. I don't tell you to fight until the last man, but to fight in order to allow the government to find a political solution. What the political solution would be I don't know.

However, despite these exhortations, the Minister of Defense said he found it difficult to get action out of the JGS. To quote General Don, the Chairman of the JGS "didn't want to do anything. . . . I pushed Cao Van Vien every morning from the day I became Minister of Defense. . . . I pushed him to use the units in the Delta, to reinforce Long An, at least south of Saigon, and reinforce maybe the 25th Division at Tay Ninh and Hau Nghia. And he told me we have a plan and so and so, and I said, 'Well, do it.' And I warned about what happened in the north. . . . If we have blame, he [Vien] is one of the persons to blame for his negative action. No coordination. No orders to anyone."

It was during the tenure of General Don that the final two military engagements of any note took place in Vietnam. These occurred at Phan Rang and Xuan Loc.

Following the evacuation of Nha Trang, the provinces of Ninh Thuan and Binh Thuan were placed under the operational control of III Corps. While Communist forces already controlled most of these two provinces, the GVN still held a portion of Phan Thiet city in Binh Thuan[42] and the airfield a few miles north of Phan Rang, the provincial capital of Ninh Thuan. Initially the Communists did not press their attack heavily in Ninh Thuan, and therefore the decision was made to reinforce the ARVN units at the Phan Rang airfield, with hopes of reoccupying the province capital, which appeared to be lightly held by Communist forces. Two

[42] According to one general officer, who was briefly in Phan Thiet, "The city was in an indescribable state of disorder, half of it was occupied by the enemy, with the rest of the city receiving heavy shelling."

240

regiments of the 2nd Division (fleshed out with Regional Force personnel) which had been withdrawn from I Corps were inserted into the airfield, along with one brigade of Airborne troops. The latter was later needed at Xuan Loc and was replaced by a Ranger group. Despite these reinforcements, Communist tanks and infantry units attacked and overran the Phan Rang airfield on April 16, after a brief but bitter struggle.

Like most GVN military operations in the final month (the major exception being Xuan Loc), the management of the Phan Rang operation was severely criticized by several respondents. General Don, who had flown to Phan Rang just before it fell, found that the JGS had failed to provide adequate logistic support to the forces there. Among other things, the JGS had sent them 105 artillery pieces "without any sights," and the units lacked "radios for the platoons to be in communication." Don considered Phan Rang an example of the "many requests for support by the unit commanders [that] were never answered by the General Staff."

Others were critical of the whole operation and questioned the motivation behind it. One respondent stated that it was "criminally poor judgment" to weakly reinforce Phan Rang with units that were so badly needed farther to the south. He further charged that the decision was influenced by the fact that Ninh Thuan was President Thieu's native province. Although other respondents also believed this to be the motivation, some considered the Phan Rang operation simply a "delaying action." If the President's motives were personal, it is indeed ironic that local troops stationed there "bulldozed and leveled" his ancestors' graves at Phan Rang in "an ultimate expression of hatred and anger."[43] In one senior officer's words, President Thieu was by then "probably the most hated man in Vietnam."

In contrast to Phan Rang, the defense of Xuan Loc was considered by all respondents to have been the high point of South Vietnamese resistance during the last days of the war. The battle at Xuan Loc had several attributes which set it apart from the previ-

---

[43] The respondent quoted here went on to state: "It was rumored that this single event was the most devastating blow to his morale and a decisive factor which caused him to resign."

ous military engagements: (1) It was the only sustained battle of division-size forces; (2) it was the one place where tactical air support was employed with significant effect; and (3) it was the one engagement where major ARVN forces stood their ground and consistently fought well.

As the provincial capital of Long Khanh, Xuan Loc controlled the important highway links to the northeast of Saigon, including the access route to the vital base at Bien Hoa. Communist units began to apply pressure around Xuan Loc on April 7, and in time some four NVA divisions were committed to battle there. Defending at Xuan Loc was ARVN's 18th Division, reinforced by one regiment of the 5th Division and the 1st Airborne Brigade. The fighting eventually became "very fierce," as the NVA used massive artillery fire and "human sea" infantry tactics to launch one assault after another against the GVN's defensive positions. The 18th Division and other defenders nevertheless held on with the help of heavy air support. C-130 transport aircraft were converted to a bombing mode and were used to drop 15,000-lb "Daisy Cutter" bombs on enemy troop concentrations. CBUs (cluster bombs) were also used with great effect at Xuan Loc and were credited by General Don as having "stopped the Communists" there. However, South Vietnam's supply of CBUs was very limited, and after it had been exhausted, the defense could no longer be sustained. Lacking further reinforcement and in danger of becoming totally surrounded, the 18th Division and other defenders were withdrawn on the 21st of April.

According to Colonel Nhan, during "14 days of fighting in Xuan Loc, SVN troops received more than 20,000 rockets and artillery shells, but they destroyed 37 Communist T-54 tanks and killed more than 5,000 Communist attackers." All the respondents manifested considerable pride in the "heroic" performance of the ARVN units defending Xuan Loc. In the words of one officer, "We could still find in our troops the An Loc fighting spirit, even a higher spirit." And Colonel Nhan reported:

> From the psychological point of view, the Xuan Loc resistance was a great help to relieve the extremely agitated mental state of the

people and soldiers. It brought back the courage and self-confidence in military commanders whose guilt complex was torturing them after the rout from the central highlands. The heroic resistance at Xuan Loc revived everyone's hope that finally the South Vietnam troops could stop the enemy aggression and thwart the enemy offensive as they had done in 1968 and 1972.

However, this was not to be, as Xuan Loc was the last significant battle of the Vietnam war.

Despite last-minute attempts to establish some sort of defense perimeter around the Saigon area, the remaining ARVN forces were no longer capable of sustaining a coherent defense against the vastly superior Communist forces pressing in on the capital. The Minister of Defense reported that he saw little further significant military action from defending forces after the loss of Xuan Loc, a situation he attributed in part to the fact that there was no coordination of the defense . . . "not only the defense, but all the battles from the beginning to the end."

One military option, apparently discussed informally by a number of officers, was to withdraw the remaining GVN forces to the Delta and continue the resistance from there. Under this concept, all the bridges from the Mekong River north would have been destroyed and the GVN would have defended from Can Tho south. As Colonel Loi explained the scheme:

> We planned to move everything to Can Tho and try to hold the Delta—and set up a kind of resistance movement and stay there in the Can Tho area, the only area we can hold because Hanoi cannot move tanks and heavy equipment down in this area.

It was his view that "if we move some troops down to the Delta and destroy all the bridges from the north, with the help from the population, the Hoa Hao, and all," it would have been possible to hold the Can Tho area for some time. However, there is no evidence that such a plan got beyond the informal discussion stage or was ever seriously considered by the JGS.[44]

[44] The Capital Military District Commander doubted that such a withdrawal to the Delta would have been a "realistic plan."

The lack of serious attention given to a withdrawal to the Delta was partly the result of the political paralysis that gripped Vietnam upon the resignation of President Thieu. On April 21, Thieu unexpectedly convened a meeting of the Council of Ministers, the first held since the fall of Ban Me Thuot, and resigned office in favor of his Vice President, Tran Van Huong. In his resignation speech, Thieu said that he was stepping down "in order to prove that it wasn't really because of him that the U.S. Government no longer afforded military assistance in Vietnam."[45] Some respondents believed that Thieu had been finally forced out at least partly as a result of American pressure. According to Bui Diem, "Thieu's resignation completely paralyzed the government which was already half paralyzed by the disastrous losses: Pleiku, Kontum, Hue, and Danang." Because of this disruption, the Minister of Defense felt the resignation was ill-timed:

> If he had to resign, it should have been a long time before, or never. Because when he resigned we met many difficulties. First, the government had to resign. There is nobody to work. His loyal followers and all key people in all units of administration also tried to follow him, tried to escape—disorder everywhere and, with the new, Tran Van Huong, he moved slowly, very slowly and he didn't give specific orders to the troops to fight until the last day, the last hour.

While several respondents considered the new President a "true patriot," they did not view him to be an effective leader in the crisis facing Vietnam. Former Prime Minister Can, who had also resigned, stated: "All that President Huong did in those couple of days he led the country was to have endless conversations with U.S. and French Ambassadors and Vietnamese top politicians, who all tried to convince him to resign for he was not accepted by Hanoi as an interlocutor." The new President also spent much of his time personally reviewing visa applications from Vietnamese seeking to leave the country. Apparently outraged by the corrupt practices involved in granting exit visas, Huong wanted to decide each case himself.

[45] As reported by Buu Vien.

Since the beginning of April, there had been a steady movement of persons out of Vietnam, some with U.S. help. In the words of Prime Minister Can, "Everybody was impatient to escape before the worst would occur like Danang, where soldiers and civilians mobbed planes and ships to get aboard." According to Can, even before he had become Prime Minister, "all banks were crowded with customers drawing out their deposits, and the immigration office, friendly embassies, the DAO, the U.S. AID offices were full of people seeking papers to get out of the country."

During the final days, Saigon was rife with rumors. Many Vietnamese still believed that the Americans would find some kind of solution. Colonel Loi reported that:

> Even the week before the fall of Saigon . . . there were rumors that there had been a coup d'état in Hanoi. Giap had been killed and that the order to the Northern divisions was to withdraw to the North. Rumors that the Chinese had moved into North Vietnam and all the Northern divisions had to go back to the North to face the Chinese. Even at the last day at Saigon, everyone thought that this was an American coup because they had the power to do something like this.

Other Vietnamese believed that the collapse itself was perpetrated by the Americans. Again according to Colonel Loi, they thought there was "an overall agreed plan with the North Vietnamese and this was carried out very closely by the Americans." The rationale of this rumor was that the "Americans want to get rid of the Vietnam problem. And secondly, they have already agreed with the North Vietnamese on something in the future. Some plan for the future for all of Indochina. So they want to get rid of the Saigon regime and do something in the future." And there were those who still hoped for American intervention: "They can intervene or they can work out some measure with China and Russia and find out some solution. And the advance of the Communist troops was just to carry out the plan that you had already set up. But we still believed that the Americans can control the situation and they can do what they want. I think that a lot of people believed this."

The most prevalent rumors, however, were about the "Big

Minh Solution.'' General Duong Van Minh had been said for years to be the only South Vietnamese leader acceptable to the Communists, and the people were waiting for him to replace President Huong and start negotiations with the Communists. In the words of General Don, "His name was in the mouth of everyone, now, as the next leader, the next solution. Nobody wants to fight because [there are] too many rumors about the Big Minh Solution, about Mr. Huong wanting to resign, and so forth. You realize now the atmosphere in Saigon at that time. If we find some units still fighting we must be grateful to these people.''

Much of the speculation about the Big Minh Solution was fired and given credibility by the attempts of the French Embassy in Saigon to play a "middleman between the parties" during the last two weeks of the war. According to Bui Diem, these activities stirred hope as to the possibility of a negotiated settlement during "these difficult days when a semblance of hope was hope.'' Bui Diem continued:

> About two weeks before the war was over, the French Ambassador in Saigon, Mr. Merillon, hinted in his conversations with the political leaders in the capital that he had contact with the Communist side. Perhaps with the tacit approval and encouragement from his government, he let it be known that the Communists might eventually accept a coalition government as a first step toward a peace settlement. Mr. Merillon apparently thought that his efforts would result in an advantageous position for France after the Communist takeover and consequently tried hard to play the role of negotiator. Openly advocating the Big Minh Solution he indicated to whomever he talked to that the only remaining obstacles on the road to peace were Mr. Thieu and his government. The Communists for their part did not discourage these behind the scenes French maneuvers. Instead they used the maneuvers to their own advantage and concentrated all their efforts into accelerating their military march on the capital.

Big Minh did indeed come to power on April 28, but a "solution" was no longer in the cards. The American airlift to evacuate U.S. and Vietnamese nationals had already been under way for several days, and Communist units were pressing in on Saigon. The new President Minh appealed to the other side to cease hostilities and attempted to start negotiations by asking the Americans to evacuate all military personnel. The Communists reacted by strafing the Presidential Palace and bombing Tan Son Nhut airport with aircraft captured from VNAF. As Buu Vien put it, "That was their pointed response to Minh's proposal." And then "shortly after midnight of April 28, the Communists began to pour heavy artillery into Tan Son Nhut airport, killing two U.S. Marines, the last to die in the Vietnam war, and interdicting any further use of the airbase. The collapse of Saigon was imminent and the U.S. Embassy ordered the final and hasty evacuation by helicopters."

Even at this last moment, however, there were still some Vietnamese who wanted to resist. Lieutenant General Vinh Loc volunteered to become the Chairman of the JGS to replace General Vien, who had left on April 28. Colonel Nhan volunteered to assist Vinh Loc in attempting to stabilize the military situation. Contact was made with local military units. In Nhan's words:

> All encouraged us and offered suggestions to stabilize the situation . . . many units reinstated their old commander. Many deputy officers took responsibilities of commanders whose whereabouts were not known. Some Armored, Airborne and Ranger units requested to be placed under the direct JGS control and seek new missions because they had lost contact with their immediate headquarters.

Plans were drawn up for counterattack, and the logistic command estimated "that it could supply gasoline and ammunition for the next 15 days if the depots were not lost to the enemy." However, these last desperate efforts came to naught when, on the morning of April 30, President Minh decided to unconditionally surrender to the Communists. Colonel Nhan described his reaction to this event:

> This news caught me by surprise because up to that moment, the JGS had never been consulted on such an important matter. Gen-

eral Loc and we had done all we could to reestablish the vitality of the disintegrating Armed Forces. The troops were regaining confidence and got ready for the fight to defend the country. But we were betrayed by the cowardly and naive politicians who choose reconciliation as their objective. They did not realize that they had no capacity to cope with the Communists who only used war and peace as a means to achieve their political goal of establishing a Communist regime in South Vietnam. . . . Now that the government had decided to surrender, [the] armed forces could no longer exist.

Chapter 15

Perceptions of the Evacuation

Perceptions of the Evacuation

While only a few respondents commented in any detail on the evacuation from Vietnam, there were several who were critical of the U.S. evacuation effort, believing that it had started too soon and, as a result, had helped undermine the will to resist.

General Tran Van Don, for example, attributed the rapid collapse of Phan Thiet to the premature evacuation of the families of senior Vietnamese officers:

> I heard that some families from the generals, colonels, were evacuated already. . . . And I tried at my meetings with the generals to ask them, "Don't be in a hurry to do it. Don't try to do it." And no response. I thought that they understood. That is all. But I knew after that when I was in Guam and Fort Chafee and I understood now why some families were evacuated one week or ten days before, families from the generals, families from the colonels, families from the pilots of the Air Force. Families from the Marines at Vung Tau. I understood when I meet some people why they were not very excited to fight. If their families went away already, the only thing to do was follow them. I know some planes had left already. I don't say all. And the lower officers, the NCOs, knew already.

Another senior officer, General Thinh, considered the early evacuation of orphans to the United States to have been a visible manifestation of "American abandonment," causing "South Vietnamese morale to be shaken." He extended this criticism to the evacuation of Americans as well:

251

At the same time as the evacuation of the orphans, there was the evacuation of the Americans themselves, beginning at the end of March 1975, of those whose presence in South Vietnam was not absolutely required. This hasty evacuation, done at the moment that provinces were falling one after the other to the enemy, had the effect of inciting most Vietnamese to leave Vietnam, if possible. It spread fear among those who saw their futures as uncertain and cloudy. It was partly responsible for the suddenness of the country's fall.

Another general who served on the JGS said he was also disturbed by the fact that the United States moved out families of senior officers first; he believed this hurt the morale of those remaining. He implied that there may have been some kind of ulterior motive—a "political decision" on the part of the United States to hurry South Vietnamese leaders outside the country. He referred to "an exaggeration of the situation" by the U.S. Defense Attaché's Office and the CIA and stated that he personally felt the Americans were trying to "hurry him" out of the country.

Former Ambassador Bui Diem, however, directed his comments to an entirely different point, suggesting that too many Vietnamese had been left behind:

> In terms of military operation within the time frame imposed by the circumstances at that time, it was perhaps a success because in less than 24 hours thousands of Americans and South Vietnamese had been evacuated under precarious conditions and with only two Marines killed during the bombing of the Tan Son Nhut airport just one day before the operation began. In terms of human tragedy and from the South Vietnamese point of view, it was another story. Hundreds of thousands of South Vietnamese who had put all their hopes in being evacuated are now suffering inside Communist jails and camps. Thousands of others who were evacuated in haste are condemned to live separated from the other members of their families without any hope of being reunited. Obviously, by the time the Communists had their advance units around Saigon, the situation was difficult for the Americans. How many South Vietnamese were to be included in the evacuation? Could it be started while the Saigon government was still operating, moribund as it

was? How about the shock effect on the population? Could panic be avoided? To all these questions there were no easy answers but somehow through lack of clear cut decisions from Washington (according to the testimony of Ambassador Martin before the House Committee on International Relations, January 1976) the U.S. Mission in Saigon got the authority to evacuate 50,000 South Vietnamese only four days before the final collapse. Lack of coordination, confusion and loss of control ensued and in the end thousands of South Vietnamese of high risk were left behind, defenseless in the hands of the Communists. They were promised help by the representatives of the U.S. Mission but at the last minute those who had promised help did not show up. Thousands of others who could well have stayed behind without too much risk were evacuated instead because they had some American good friend who claimed them as relatives, or in many cases, simply because they succeeded in getting in touch with some of the American adventurers who unscrupulously organized the evacuation for their own profit.

Many evacuees are crippled by the simple fact that they had to leave South Vietnam and try to start a new life in another country far away from their ancestral land with no practical hope of coming home. And by the way the whole program was carried out, the evacuation was sad, even heartbreaking for many South Vietnamese.

In concluding, Bui Diem noted that "the whole operation was in a way an unhappy ending for an unhappy chapter of American history and the Americans can quickly turn the page; but for all the South Vietnamese, whether they stayed in South Vietnam or succeeded in going abroad, the war and the evacuation was a continuing nightmare. For them, the tragic scenes of those South Vietnamese families at dawn on the roofs of the buildings in downtown Saigon, waiting anxiously but hopelessly for the blinking lights of a helicopter which never came back, or the scenes of those innumerable barges and sampans rushing eastward into the high sea with the hazardous expectation of being rescued by the U.S. Seventh Fleet will be remembered for all time to come."

The Collapse in Retrospect: Some Final Questions

The Collapse in Retrospect: Some Final Questions

After all that has been said, there still remains a final set of questions about the fall of South Vietnam: Could the outcome have been different? Did our South Vietnamese respondents see the collapse as inevitable, and if not, what might have been done to avert the disaster?

As to the latter question, there is consensus among the respondents on one point: Had the Americans not "abandoned" Vietnam, the course of events would have been quite different. Most respondents agreed that an effective defense could have been sustained for some time had U.S. aid not been cut back after the Paris Agreements. Most also believed that the reintervention of U.S. airpower, especially B-52s, would have prevented defeat in 1975. None would contend that continued aid or renewed intervention would have ended the war or brought victory—significantly, the word "victory" does not appear in the interviews.

But beyond this fundamental conviction that U.S. support was crucial, the views of the respondents on "what might have been done" become more diffuse and complex, and must in part be distilled through inference. While some respondents offered explicit suggestions about what they believed to have been more promising options for the conduct of the war, the views of most must be drawn from the catalog of reasons they cited for the collapse. These range over a wide field: South Vietnam's armed forces were poorly led, stretched too thin, lacked an efficient general staff, and were improperly organized to cope with the threat at hand. It was difficult to mobilize national resources and impose the discipline necessary to fight a long war within the

257

democratic norms the South was obliged to follow. Corruption was rampant. North Vietnam, by contrast, was a totalitarian society, geared for war, fully supported by its allies, and after 1973, free from direct attack, even in its southern sanctuaries.

The major points made included the following: Thieu should have been removed, along with, by implication, the corrupt and incompetent people he appointed. South Vietnam's territory should have been consolidated to make it more defensible. A more austere style of fighting should have been adopted. Manpower policies should have been changed. More divisions should have been activated. A coherent strategy for conducting the war should have been developed, along with more viable contingency plans in the event of a full-scale offensive. South Vietnam should have attacked the North, or at least harassed the enemy's lines of communication in the South. South Vietnam should have tried to hold out longer.

Although few said so directly, the respondents implied that had at least some of these and other things been done, the outcome of the war would have been different, which suggests that they felt defeat was not inevitable. But they did none of these things. One reason given for this is that such actions would have required America's acquiescence, if not its active support—after all, it was America that had insisted on the maintenance of democratic norms, organized the ARVN in the image of the U.S. Army, and refused to equip additional divisions. Moreover, South Vietnam's leaders seemed convinced that such painful reforms were in fact unnecessary, because the Americans could be counted on to bail out the South in an emergency.

But there was also one other fundamental factor that discouraged reform: None of South Vietnam's weaknesses seemed solvable in isolation; rather, each was part of an intricate web. According to this view, the causes of the collapse were so "inextricably interwoven" that no single change in the conduct of the war on their part alone would have affected the outcome and, in any case, they considered most reforms to be difficult, if not impossible to realize. (In contrast, American officials generally tended to consider South Vietnam's weaknesses to be discrete and individually remediable problems.) Change in South Vietnam often faced a vicious circle. It seemed impossible, for example, to get competent military commanders because of the corruption in the promotion system. Yet it was impossible to clean up corruption without concerted action on the part of President Thieu, who was himself in on or at least a "captive" of the system. But it was risky to get rid of Thieu because only he had the support of the Americans, and without American support the South Vietnamese could not carry on the war.

Thus, the principal causes of the disaster were seen as all interacting upon one another at any given time and encompassing a wide spectrum of military, social, political, and international factors. They embodied a composite of past errors, weaknesses, and misperceptions that left South Vietnam inherently vulnerable to an enemy superior in will and power.

Although it would be wrong to conclude that the South Vietnamese saw themselves as entirely helpless, they tended to see themselves as being "moved" rather than being "movers." This theme comes through quite strongly in the interviews. It appears first in their perceptions of how America was able to impose its will on Vietnam: In their view, the Americans, while they may not have been the architects of defeat, greatly contributed to it by simultaneously pushing for a vast range of different and irreconcilable objectives, more or less from the beginning of the war. The push for greater South Vietnamese military strength was incompatible with the push to encourage greater democracy and freedom. The Americans wanted the South Vietnamese government to create a broader political base and reduce corruption, but they continued to back Thieu. The Americans gave the South Vietnamese a military machine that was inherently costly to maintain and operate, and then wanted them to reduce military costs and operate with far less aid. The Americans wanted South Vietnam to demobilize men to transfer them to the civilian economy, while the enemy was increasing its military strength. This attempt to build a political and economic showcase in the midst of a hard war was regarded as unrealistic, and some South Vietnamese officials apparently felt squeezed—or in some cases suspended—between high-flown American plans and harsh military, economic, and political realities.

But the perception of being "moved" was reflected more fundamentally by those who saw South Vietnam to be but one piece of a larger contest. They viewed the war not simply as a conflict between themselves and the North Vietnamese but as part of a global struggle between the Soviet Union and China on the one side and the free world, led by the United States, on the other. In such a struggle, the will and the actions of the South Vietnamese could have but limited impact; the Americans held the real power. The course of the war and its outcome would depend on events and decisions made in a higher arena, and it was there they were to be ultimately failed. Détente with the Soviet Union and the rapprochement with China, together with the American President's Watergate troubles and America's inherent "impatience" (a condition they contrasted with their enemies' unlimited willingness to endure), combined to erode the desire and capacity of the United States to further resist Communist expansion.

Thus, the destiny of South Vietnam, in the final analysis, was regarded to have rested in the hands of others—and in this sense was a matter of fate, which, after all, is a concept deeply embedded in Vietnamese culture. And, as one respondent concluded, "Fate was not on our side."

Index

264

Selected Rand Books

Becker, Abraham S. *Soviet National Income 1958-64*. Berkeley & Los Angeles: University of California Press, 1969.

Brewer, Garry D. and Martin Shubik. *The War Game: A Critique of Military Problem Solving*. Cambridge, Mass.: Harvard University Press, 1979.

Brodie, Bernard. *Strategy in the Missile Age*. Princeton, N.J.: Princeton University Press, 1959.

Davison, W. Phillips. *The Berlin Blockade: A Study in Cold War Politics*. Princeton, N.J.: Princeton University Press, 1958.

Dinerstein, H. S. *War and the Soviet Union: Nuclear Weapons and the Revolution in Soviet Military and Political Thinking*. New York: Frederick A. Praeger, 1959.

Fainsod, Merle. *Smolensk Under Soviet Rule*. Cambridge, Mass.: Harvard University Press, 1958.

Garthoff, Raymond L. *Soviet Military Doctrine*. Glencoe, Ill.: The Free Press, 1953.

George, Alexander L. *Propaganda Analysis: A Study of Inferences Made From Nazi Propaganda In World War II*. Evanston, Ill.: Row, Peterson and Company, 1959.

Goldhamer, Herbert. *The Adviser*. New York: Elsevier North-Holland, 1978.

Goldhamer, Herbert, *The Soviet Soldier: Soviet Military Management at the Troop Level*. New York: Crane, Russak & Company, Inc., 1975.

Gouré, Leon. *Civil Defense in the Soviet Union*. Los Angeles, Calif.: University of California Press, 1962.

Gouré, Leon. *The Siege of Leningrad*. Stanford, Calif.: Stanford University Press, 1962.

Gurtov, Melvin. *Southeast Asia Tomorrow: Problems and Prospects for US Policy*. Baltimore, Md.: The Johns Hopkins Press, 1970.

Halpern, Manfred. *The Politics of Social Change in the Middle East and North Africa*. Princeton, N.J.: Princeton University Press, 1963.

Hitch, Charles J., and Roland McKean. *The Economics of Defense in the Nuclear Age*. Cambridge, Mass.: Harvard University Press, 1960.

Horelick, Arnold L., and Myron Rush. *Strategic Power and Soviet Foreign Policy*. Chicago, Ill.: University of Chicago Press, 1966.

Hosmer, Stephen T. *Viet Cong Repression and Its Implications for the Future*. Lexington, Mass.: D.C. Heath and Company, 1970.

Hsieh, Alice Langley. *Communist China's Strategy in the Nuclear Era*. Englewood Cliffs, N.J.: Prentice-Hall, 1962.

Johnson, John J. (ed.). *The Role of the Military in Underdeveloped Countries*. Princeton, N.J.: Princeton University Press, 1962.

Kecskemeti, Paul. *The Unexpected Revolution*. Stanford, Calif.: Stanford University Press, 1961.

Kolkowicz, Roman. *The Soviet Military and the Communist Party*. Princeton, N.J.: Princeton University Press, 1967.

Leites, Nathan. *A Study of Bolshevism*. Glencoe, Ill.: The Free Press, 1953.

Leites, Nathan. *The Operational Code of the Politburo*. New York: McGraw-Hill Book Company, 1951.

Leites, Nathan, and Charles Wolf, Jr. *Rebellion and Authority: An Analytic Essay on Insurgent Conflicts*. Chicago, Ill.: Markham Publishing Company, 1970.

Lubell, Harold. *Middle East Oil Crises and Western Europe's Energy Supplies*. Baltimore, Md.: The Johns Hopkins Press, 1963.

Quade, E. S. *Analysis for Public Decisions*. New York: Elsevier North-Holland, 1975.

Quade, E. S., and W. I. Boucher. *Systems Analysis and Policy Planning Applications in Defense*. New York: American Elsevier Publishing Co., 1968.

Rosen, George. *Democracy and Economic Change in India*. Berkeley and Los Angeles, Calif.: University of California Press, 1966.

Rush, Myron. *Political Succession in the USSR*. New York: Columbia University Press, 1965.

Rush, Myron. *The Rise of Khrushchev*. Washington, D.C.: Public Affairs Press, 1958.

Scalapino, Robert A. *The Japanese Communist Movement, 1920-1966*. Berkeley and Los Angeles, Calif.: University of California Press, 1967.

Sokolovskii, V. D. (ed.). *Soviet Military Strategy*. Englewood Cliffs, N.J.: Prentice-Hall, 1963.

Speier, Hans. *Divided Berlin: The Anatomy of Soviet Political Blackmail*. New York: Frederick A. Praeger, 1961.

Speier, Hans, and W. Phillips Davison (eds.). *West German Leadership and Foreign Policy*. Evanston, Ill.: Row, Peterson and Company, 1957.

Tanham, G. K. *Communist Revolutionary Warfare: The Vietminh in Indochina*. New York: Frederick A. Praeger, 1961.

Whiting, Allen S. *China Crosses the Yalu: The Decision to Enter the Korean War*. New York: The Macmillan Company, 1960.

Wolf, Charles, Jr. *Foreign Aid: Theory and Practice in Southern Asia*. Princeton, N.J.: Princeton University Press, 1960.

Wolfe, Thomas W. *Soviet Power and Europe 1945-1970*. Baltimore, Md.: The Johns Hopkins Press, 1970.

Wolfe, Thomas W. *Soviet Strategy at the Crossroads*. Cambridge, Mass.: Harvard University Press, 1964.